Einar — Jamex
de la Torre

California State University, Fullerton - Main Art Gallery
Grand Central Press

Fall of Empire

a collaborative process

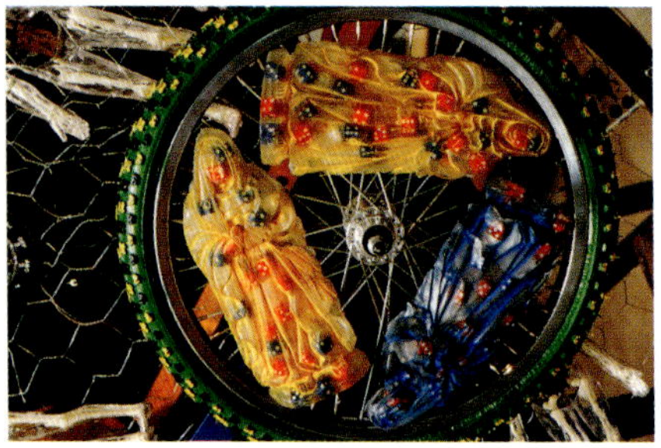

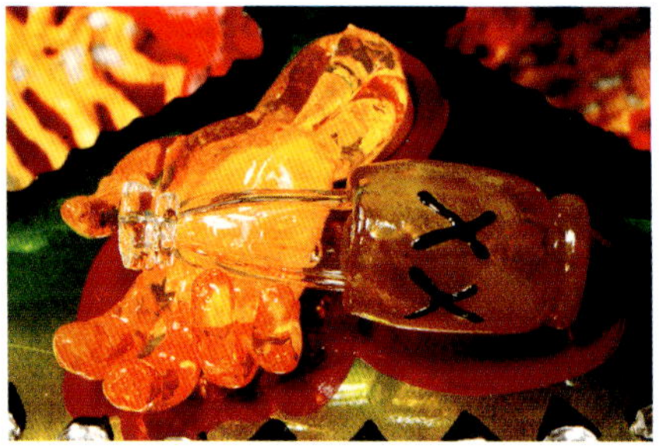

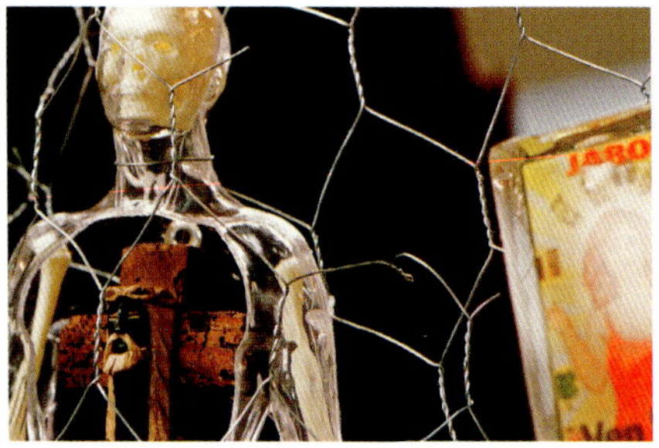

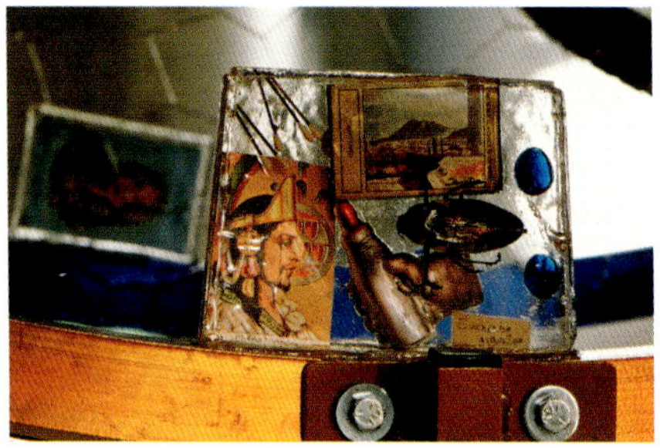

When Mike McGee asked me if I thought the de la Torre brothers would be interested in an exhibition here at Cal State Fullerton, I had to smile. The de la Torre brothers and I go way back, back to 1994, when I was putting an exhibition together in the San Francisco State Art Gallery in conjunction with the International Glass Art Society Conference. The exhibit was titled *Glass from the Pacific Rim*. I had invited artists from California, Canada, Japan, New Zealand, Australia, etc., and I asked glass artist Therman Statom if he could recommend any artists from Western Mexico. He introduced me to the de la Torre brothers, and I loved their work. We have worked together many times and in many places, from Tucson, Arizona, to Fukui, Japan. Over the years, we have become good friends. The smile was because in the past decade the de la Torres' careers have exploded. They are in such demand with museum exhibitions, teaching workshops, and working on public art projects that I didn't know if they would be able to fit us in.

During the planning of this project, we talked about how difficult it would be to mount any kind of survey exhibition or to document specific bodies of work because the artists' careers were on such a fast track. The idea that the whole project would be a kind of work in progress emerged. We decided to give the brothers free hands to combine existing, autonomous works with some kind of installation that would be produced during the first half of the spring semester. Mike and I encouraged these very busy artists to share the chaos and intensity of their professional lives with our students. We invited them to work here in our gallery and in the Art Department's Glass Studios in collaboration with Cal StateFullerton Grand Central Art Center's artists-in-residence program.

Details of *La Belle Epoch*, 2001

The whole project was designed to give students in the exhibition design and glass programs access to the entire process from design to execution and from installation to exhibition. These students had a rare opportunity to jump on the fast moving train of two fully mature artists doing what they do best, and to share the ride for a few brief weeks. We have tried to document that process, not only with the work in this gallery, which was installed with the help of Mike's exhibition design students, but also with this two-volume catalogue. In this, the first volume, we will present many of the individual autonomous works from the exhibition. Some of this work was made in the artists' studio and some was made here, with the help of my students, in our glass shop. The second volume of this catalogue, which will be available at the close of the exhibition, will contain photographic and written documentation of the semester-long residency, including interviews with some of the students and the de la Torre brothers.

Jamex and Einar de la Torre are unique in the studio glass movement. Collaborations in general are not unusual and there are many examples of family members carrying on the tradition of glass making. I can think of no other collaborative team of artists working in glass who have more consistently pushed themselves and each other toward shared goals. They share a ranch in Mexico and a studio in southern California. They travel together, they teach together and they work together. Jimmy and Einar question just about everything we think we understand about the multicultural sawdust of southern California. They continue to create a legacy of consistently powerful, provocative, complex work that is a monument to the collaborative process.

It is an honor to act as guest curator of this exhibition and to have yet another opportunity to work with these two amazing artists.

John Leighton
Curator and Glass Program Head

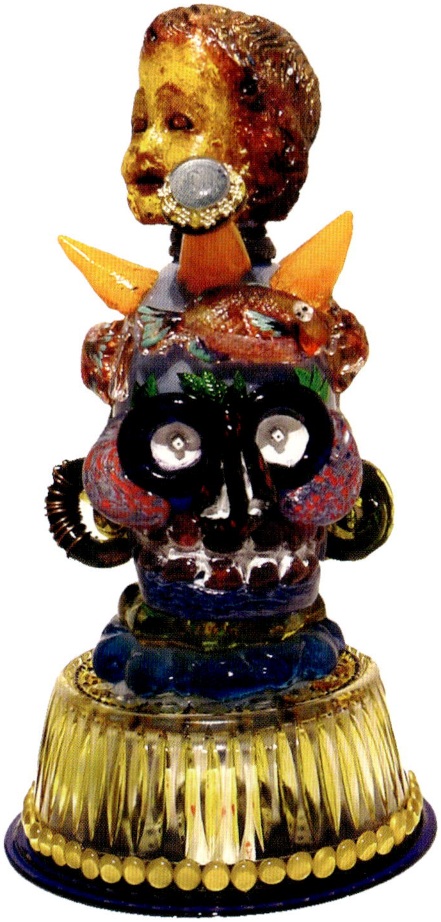

Einar and Jamex collaboration
Death of Innocence, 2001
Mixed media with blown glass
20 x 9 x 9

Wrestling with Definitions

Einar and Jamex de la Torre's art, like their lives, exists in an edgy limbo between Mexico, the U.S. and a future where global consciousness is elevated to the point where such distinctions as national citizenship will be less relevant than they are today. Their art is thick with keen-witted humor and layers of irony that target both contemporary culture and historical facts and myths.

The de la Torres are difficult to write about because so much has been written about them already and because they defy definition—both because of circumstance and a concerted effort on their part. The brothers were born to a Danish-Mexican American mother and a Mexican father in Guadalajara, Mexico, but they moved to Dana Point, California, when they were nine and twelve years old, respectively. One can only imagine the social shock of two pre-adolescent boys—who had attended an all-boys school in Mexico—being plunged into a Southern California beach city public school in 1972, just as the decade of Love and Vietnam war protests were winding down.

Einar and Jamex emerged onto the art scene about a decade ago. One of their first exhibitions was at the Orange County Center for Contemporary Art, an artists collaborative currently located across the street from the Cal State Fullerton Grand Central Art Center in Santa Ana. They had studied glass blowing at Cal State Long Beach and were labeled "glass artists," a distinction that proved increasingly flimsy as their careers unfolded.

Glass art exists in a universe unto itself, claiming its own collectors and galleries—and now, with the Tacoma Museum in Washington where the de la Torre brothers currently have their first major survey exhibition in the US, its own museum. As a genre, glass art is more than a little removed from but in many ways runs parallel to the non-glass art world. For instance, few glass collectors have extensive collections of other types of contemporary art; likewise, few noted contemporary art collectors have a significant amount of glass art in their collections.

By its very nature, glass addresses one of the contentious issues art has grappled with in the 20th century, the concept of beauty. The 19th-century notion of beauty exemplified by dandified academic paintings with their glass-like overly glazed surfaces, meticulously rendered imagery, and carefully orchestrated bright color was roundly rejected by artists in the beginning of the 20th century, especially by Dadaists and others who had emerged from World War I. The rejection resulted in a lot of Modern art that was more rough and expressive in its appearance than refined and graceful. Discourse on this issue echoed throughout the century and came to a peak in the 1990s as Dave Hickey, Arthur Danto, and others mulled it over in an expansive stream of books, essays, and panel discussions. The results of this discourse are inconclusive, but it ultimately yielded contemporary artists license to explore and investigate a broader range of esthetic possibilities.

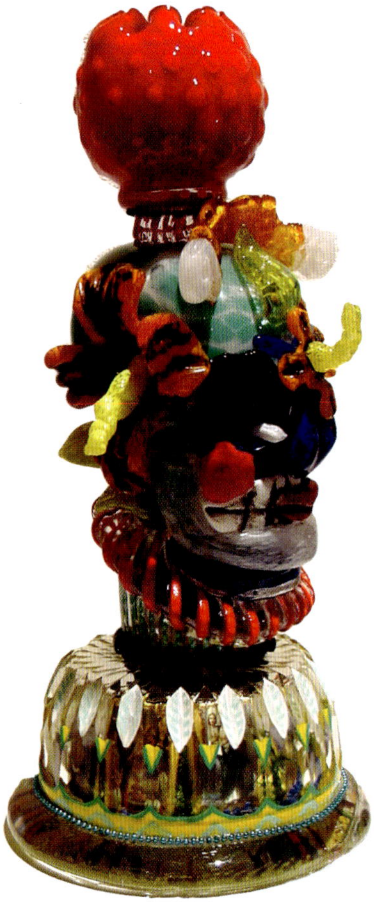

Einar and Jamex collaboration
Mamá Carlota, 2001,
Mixed media with blown glass
21 x11 x11

Right:
Einar and Jamex collaboration
The Good Ship Extasy, 2004
Mixed media with blown glass
84 x 84 x 16

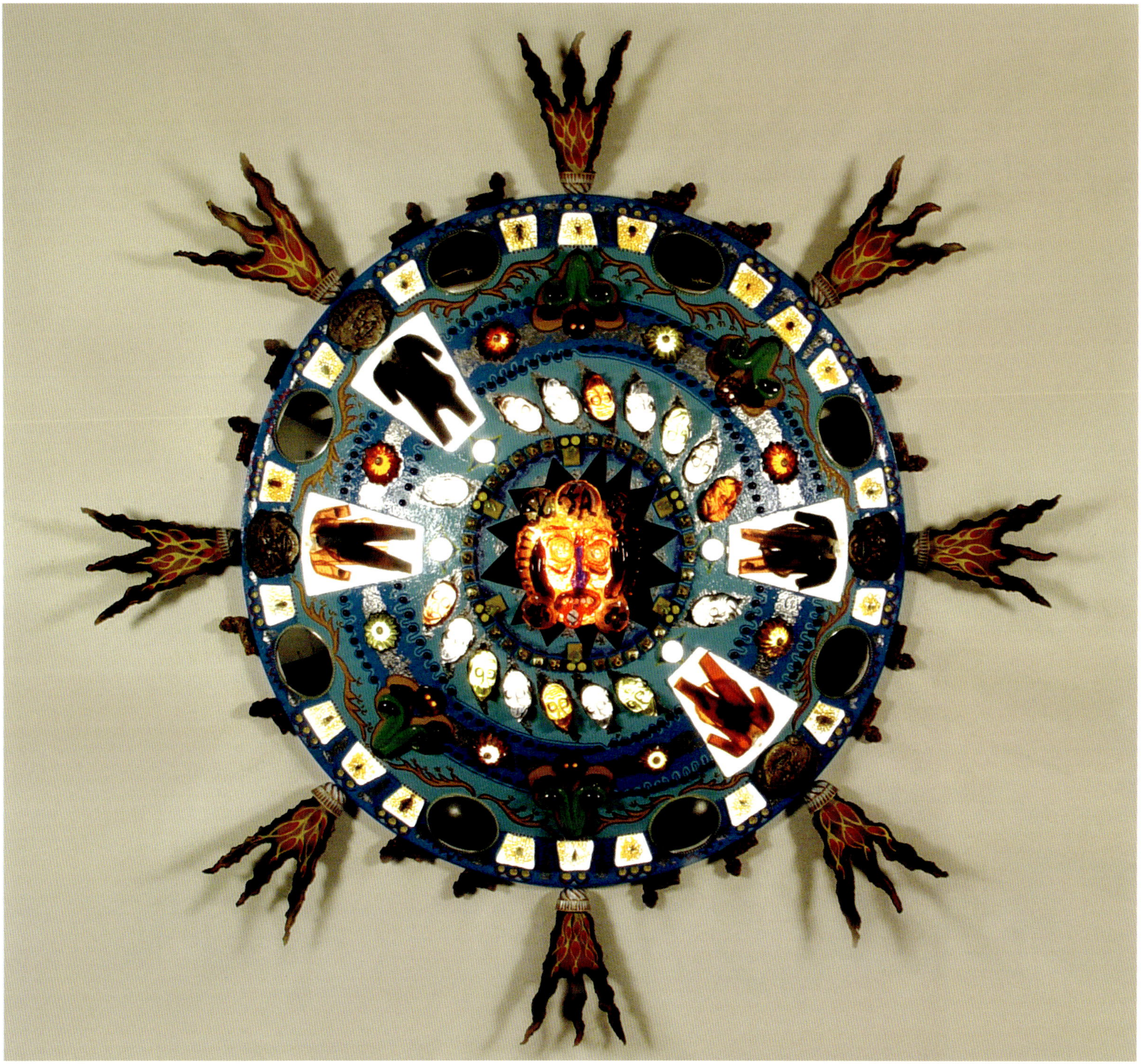

The de la Torres turn the whole beauty cart upside down by infusing the elegant sensual medium of glass with a barrage of mostly kitsch references and influences. The result is a consistently garish visual overload that assaults the senses and exponentially intensifies the many ironies with which the two artists jostle. One such irony is that they have chosen glass as their primary medium since one of the targets for their critical lampoons is the fetishistic passion with which the glass world—both artists and collectors alike—covet the medium. The de la Torres play both ends against the middle when it comes to glass, using the medium for its esthetic characteristics and then pushing those characteristics so far over the top that they become parodies.

Increasingly, the de la Torres have revealed their use of glass as more a matter of being an appropriate tool for their purpose than the obsession it is with most glass artists. They will often use other mediums, such as resin, if it better suits their needs. In *The Good Ship Extasy* (2004), for example, when they want to suspend beans and beetles in a clear, glass-like casing, they use resin. Glass just wouldn't work. Anything but purists, they routinely mix glass with a free-wheeling range of materials and objects such as faux fur, resin, paint, video, lights, liquor bottles, photographs, figurines, leather, fabrics, metal, video monitors, ceramics, trinkets, plastic flowers, coins, and dead insects just a smidgen from a constantly growing list. Installation and public art are two parts of their oeuvre rapidly growing in number. Currently working on five public art projects, the de la Torres often combine glass with other media materials. Sometimes they avoid using glass altogether.

Another classification that doesn't work neatly for either of them is that of Chicano artist. In Los Angeles they exhibit at Daniel Saxon Gallery: a small yet respected and successful gallery in West Hollywood that represents Gronk, Patsi Valdez, John Valadez, Carlos Alvarez, and other celebrated "Chicano artists." If you talk to Einar and Jamex, you'll learn that they don't feel comfortable with this or any other classification, and that their work does not focus on the usual Chicano issues.

Chicano art is routinely proud of its Mexican heritage, focusing on struggles and issues encountered by immigrants, especially those living in East Los Angeles, an epicenter for Mexican culture. The de la Torres' center of gravity is broader and, if anything, focused more south of the border or, perhaps, on the border itself. Einar says, "We see it as a matter of wearing different hats— Mexican, American, Mexican-American, Chicano, Border. . . . we prefer not to be self-defined in order to have the freedom to do anything we might want to do without labels getting in the way."

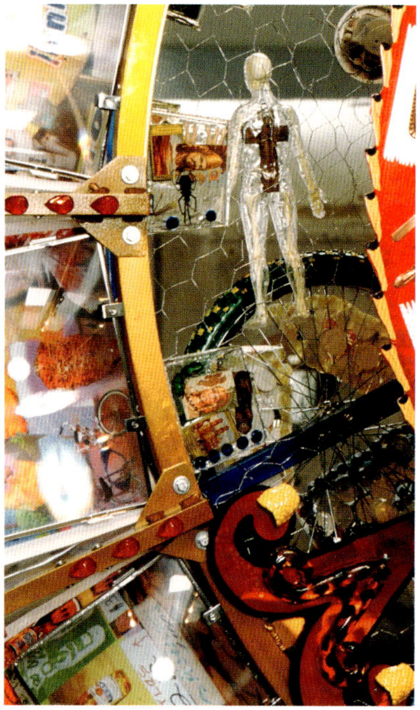

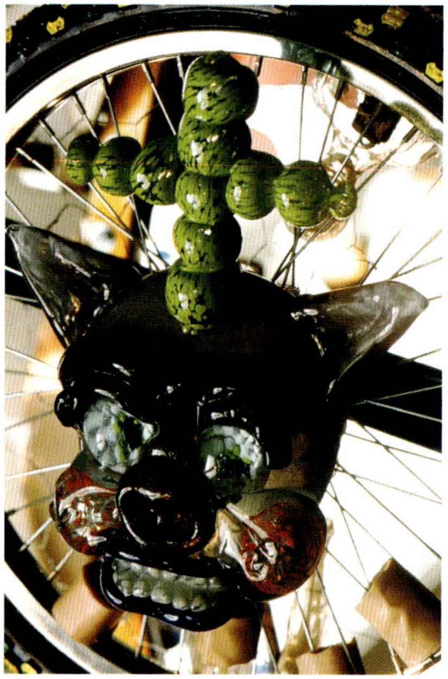

Details of *La Belle Epoch*, 2001

The humor in the de la Torres' art, however, has a distinctly Mexican flavor, a sense of humor that often has more than a little sting to it. Much Mexican humor centers around a prevailing sense that the world is a mess, that it's a by-product of the human condition, that there is little we can do to fix or overcome it as individuals, and that the best way to deal with it is to poke fun at everything in it, including ourselves. For the de la Torres, there is plenty of fodder for their humor, and, as is the case with much Mexican humor, there is frequently an underlying seriousness to it. They load their work with visual and literal references—Mexican wrestlers, Olmec figures, Aztec traditions, colonialism, capitalism, Catholicism, and Puritanism. These are just a few topics they enjoy combining with playful allusions to language—especially translations between English and Spanish—a combination of outrageous juxtapositions, visual puns, and satirical characterizations.

An example of this combination is *It's in the Cards* (2005), a cadmium yellow faux fur-covered panel onto which the de la Torres have mounted nine blown-glass human hearts, each with a word in Spanish hand-written in script on the surface. The image of the human heart has a long-standing history in Mexican culture that goes all the way back to the Aztec ritual of human sacrifice, which the de la Torres see as only a slightly removed kin of the Conquistadores' Catholicism-justified use of human massacre. The words suggest reasons why, according to the artists, one might die. One heart bears the word "Tonto," the name of the Lone Ranger's sidekick. In Spanish it means idiot.

With so many dichotomies afoot in the artists' work, it is appropriate that the catalog for this exhibition is published in two volumes, much in the same fashion that the exhibition *Fall of Empire* is divided into two parts. The first volume of the catalog and the first part of the exhibition feature a sampling of recent and past works. The second volume documents the process and glass- blowing techniques of the de la Torres in general and, especially, the development of the site-specific installation they are creating for this exhibition. It is a mock documentation of empires, and leaders of empires, that have fallen or, in the case of George W. and in the minds of the de la Torres, are in the process of falling.

Mike McGee, Director
Cal State Fullerton Main Art Gallery

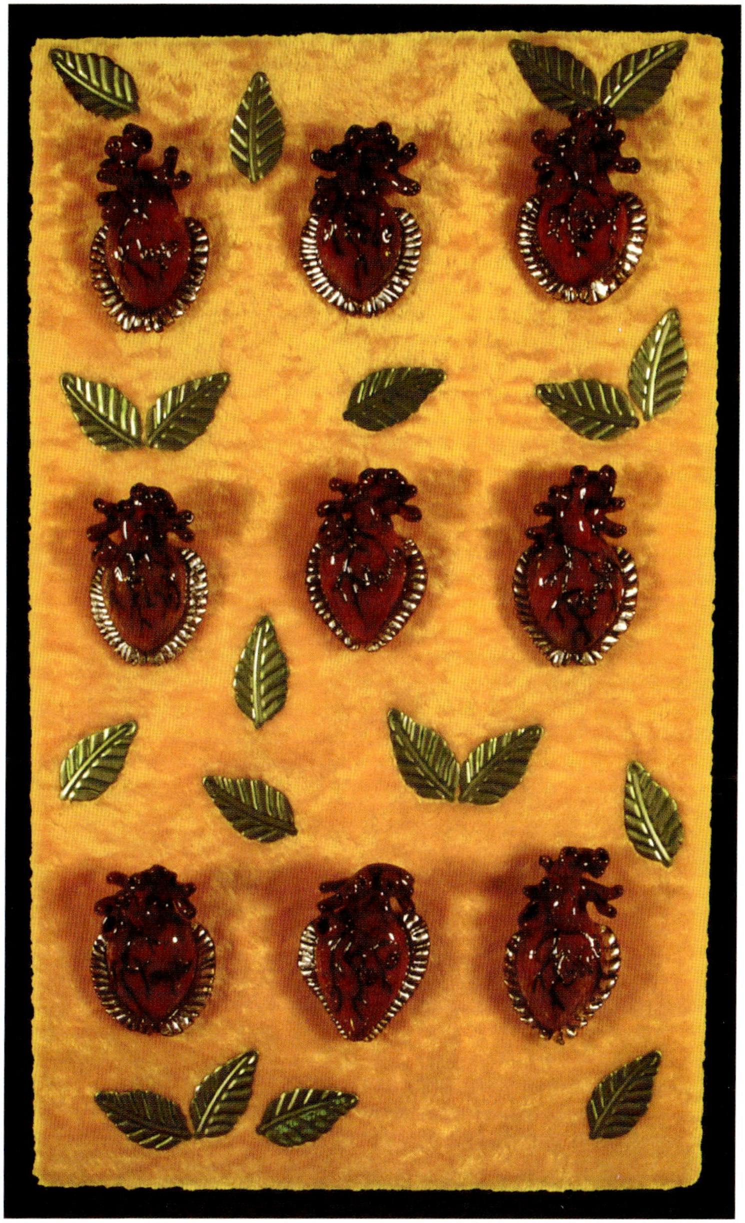

Einar and Jamex collaboration
It's in the Cards, 2005
Mixed media with blown glass
48 x 30 x 5

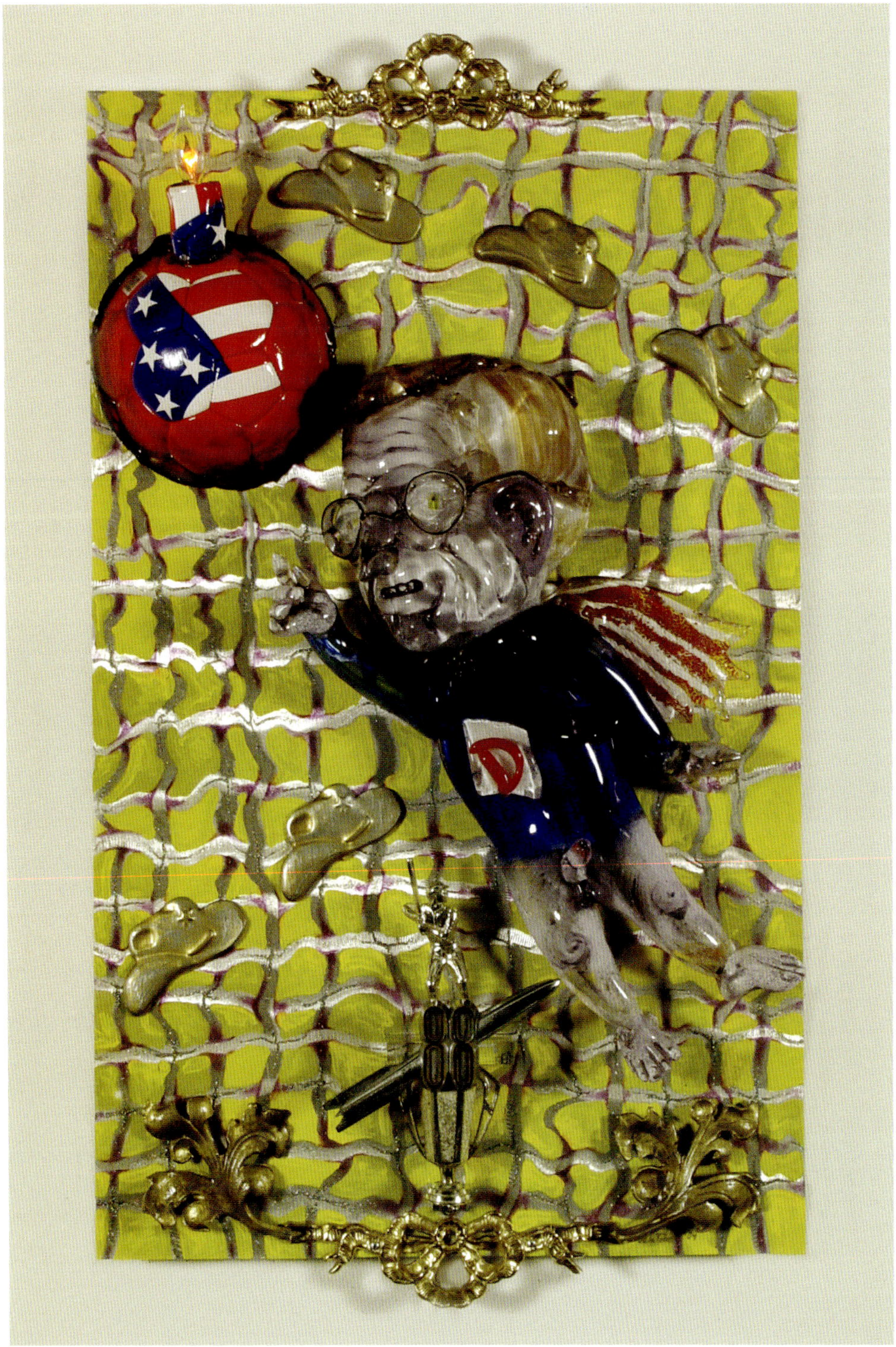

Einar and Jamex collaboration
Act Patriot, 2004
Mixed media with blown glass
40 x 23 x 7

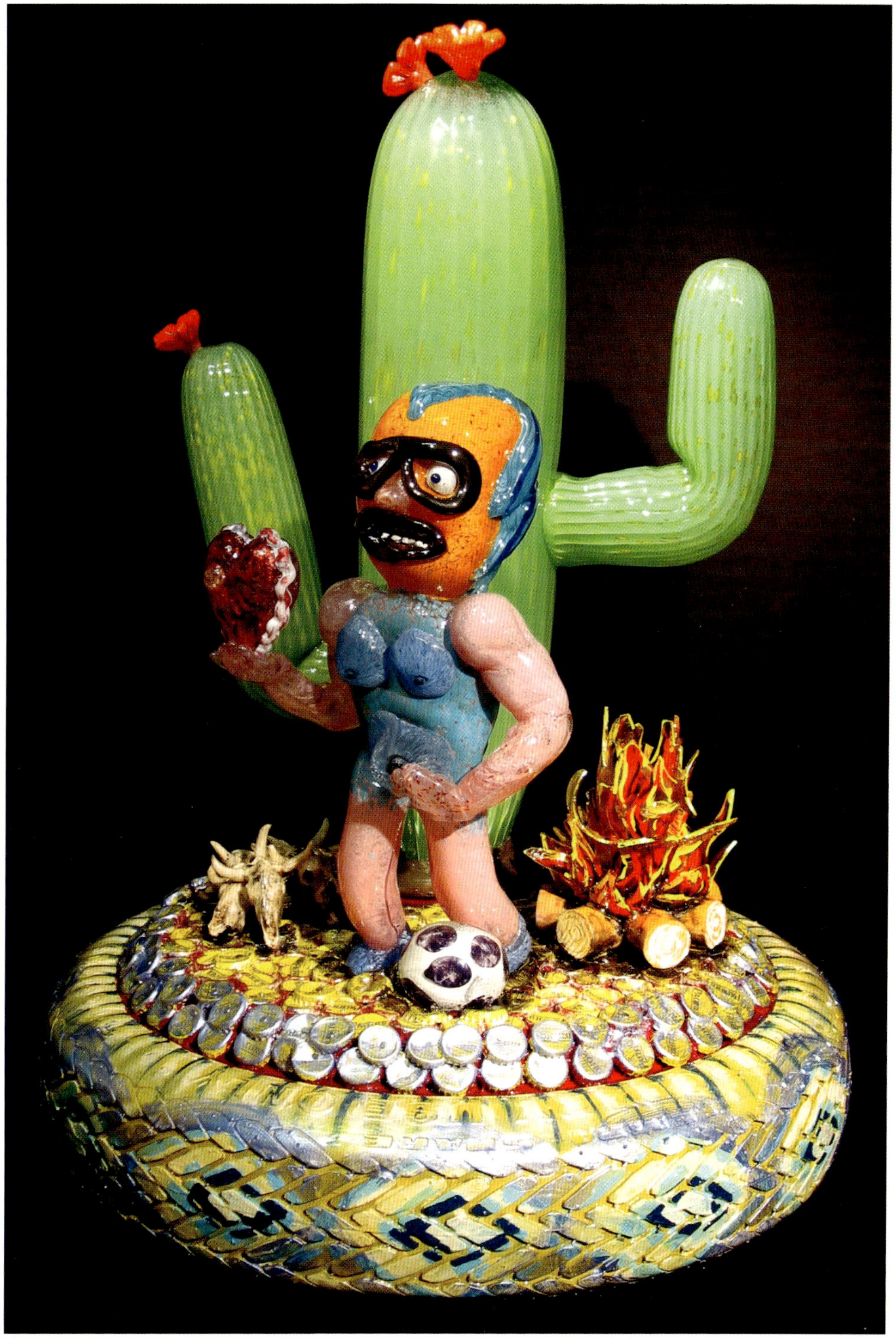

Einar and Jamex collaboration
The Desert Blooms, 2004
Mixed media with blown glass
33 x 24 x 24

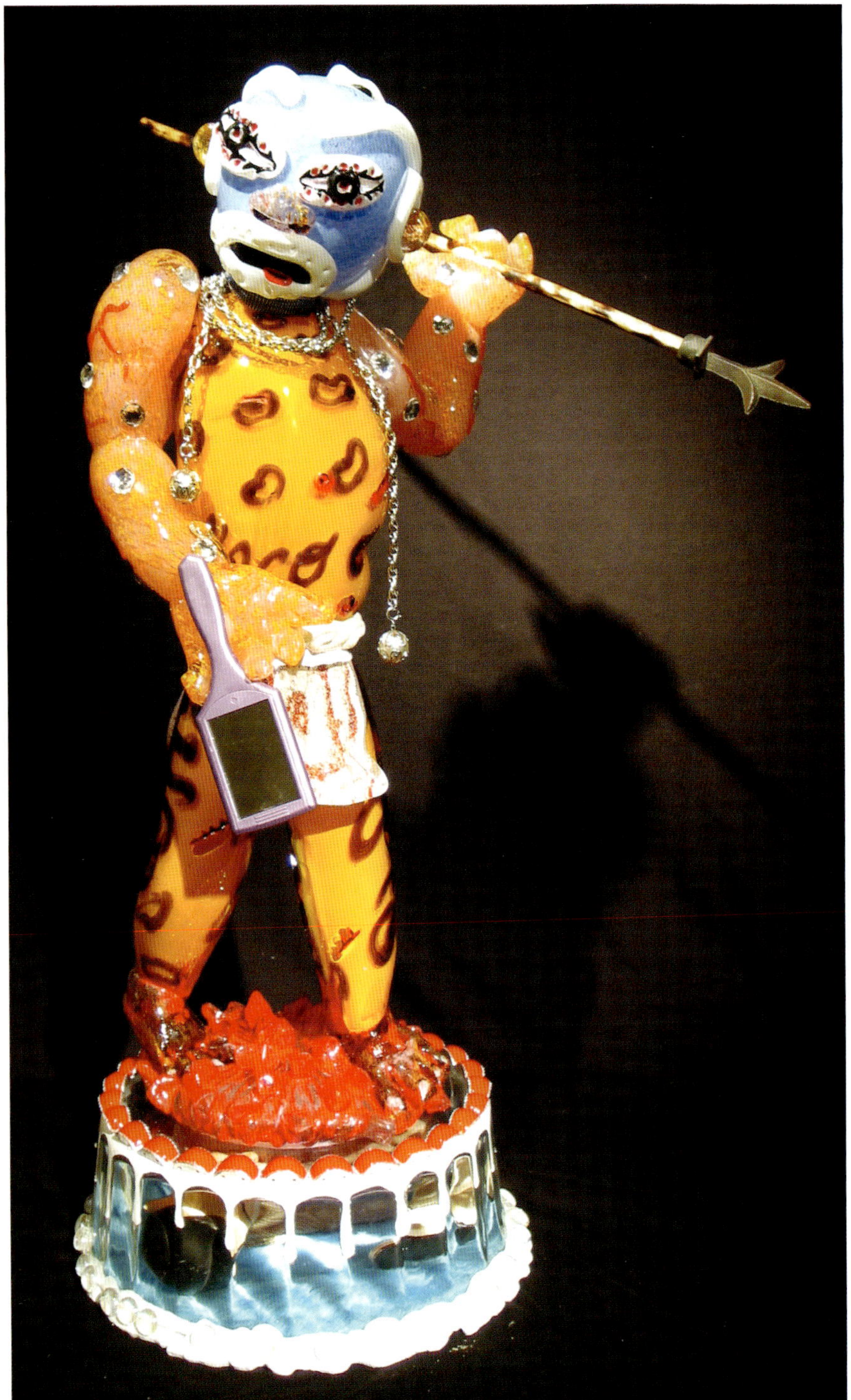

Einar and Jamex collaboration
Killing the Inner Child, 2004
Mixed media with blown glass
36 x 17 x 18

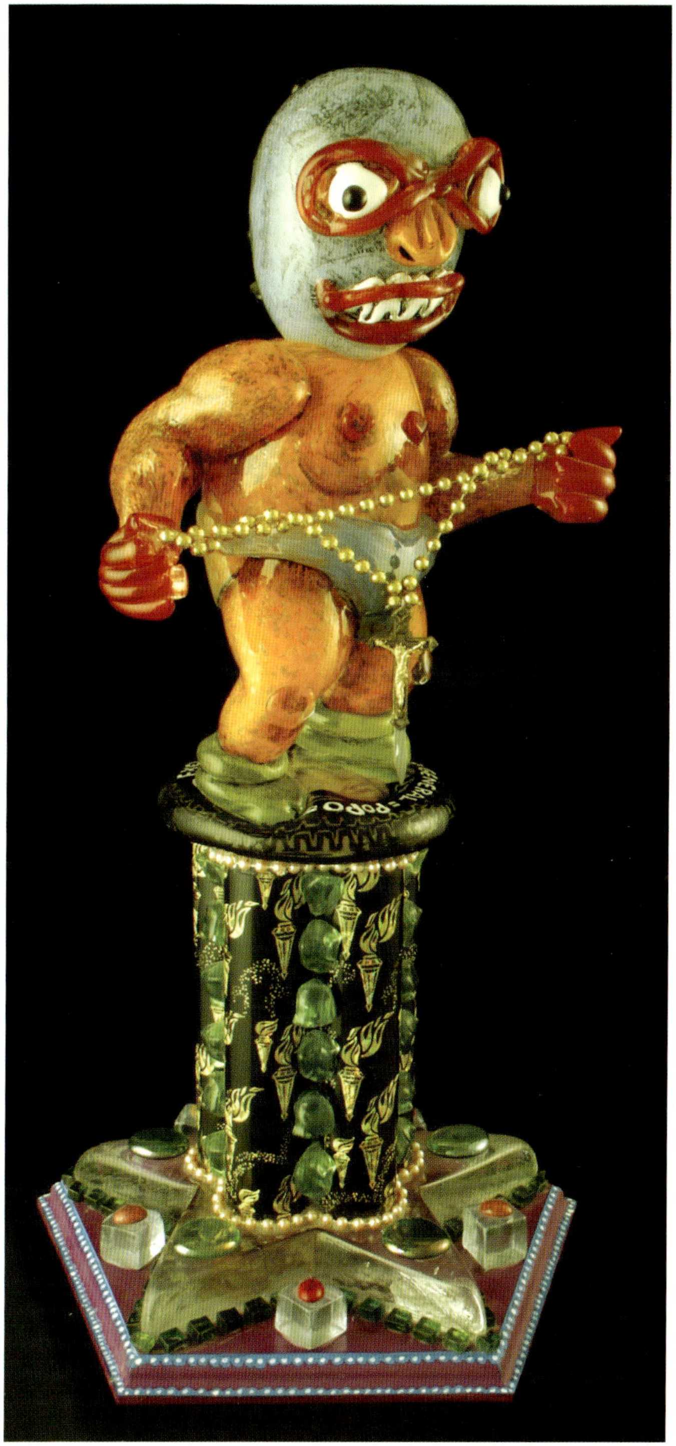

Einar and Jamex collaboration
El Luchadorcito, 2004
Mixed media with blown glass
24 x 12 x 11

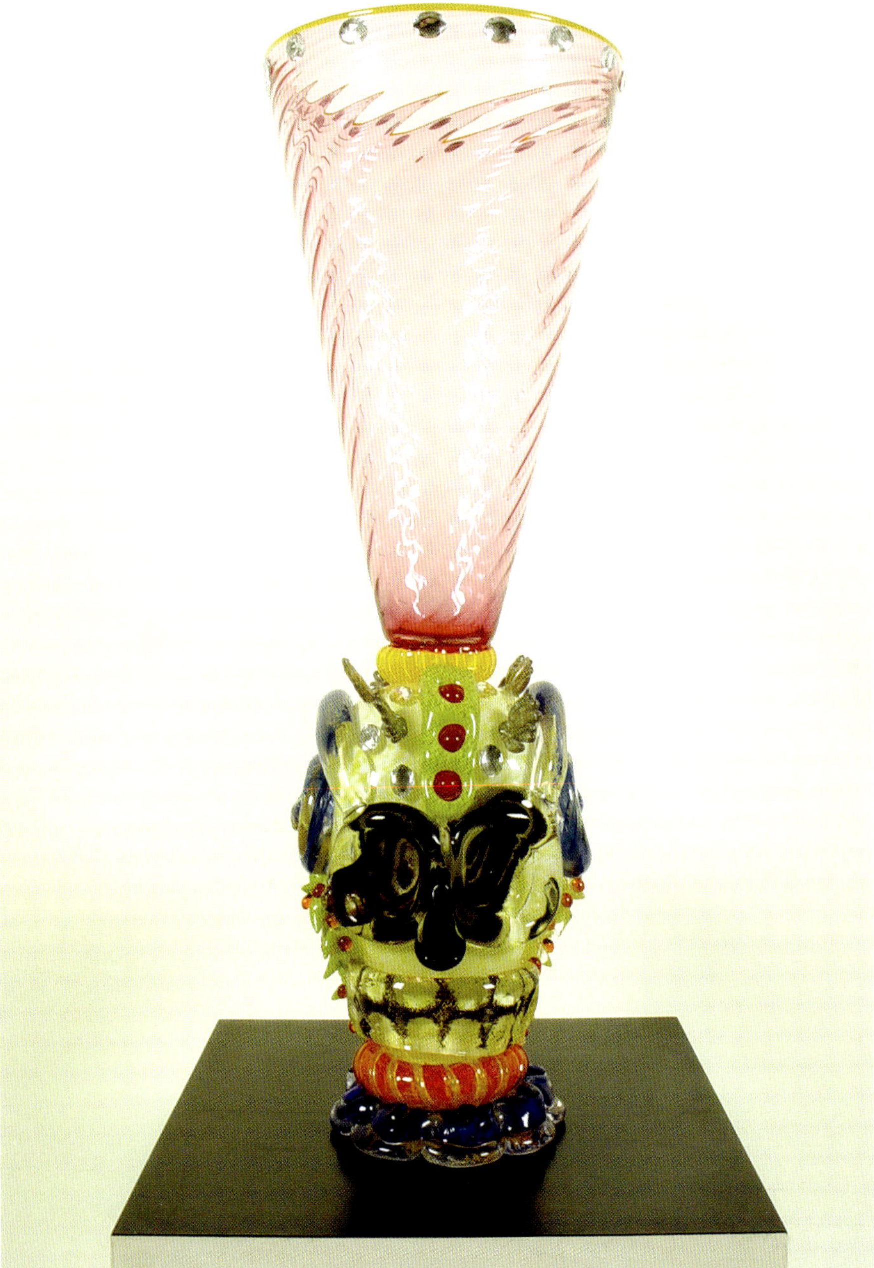

Einar and Jamex collaboration
Calavera del Tornado , 2005
Mixed media with blown glass
32.5 x 9 x 10.5

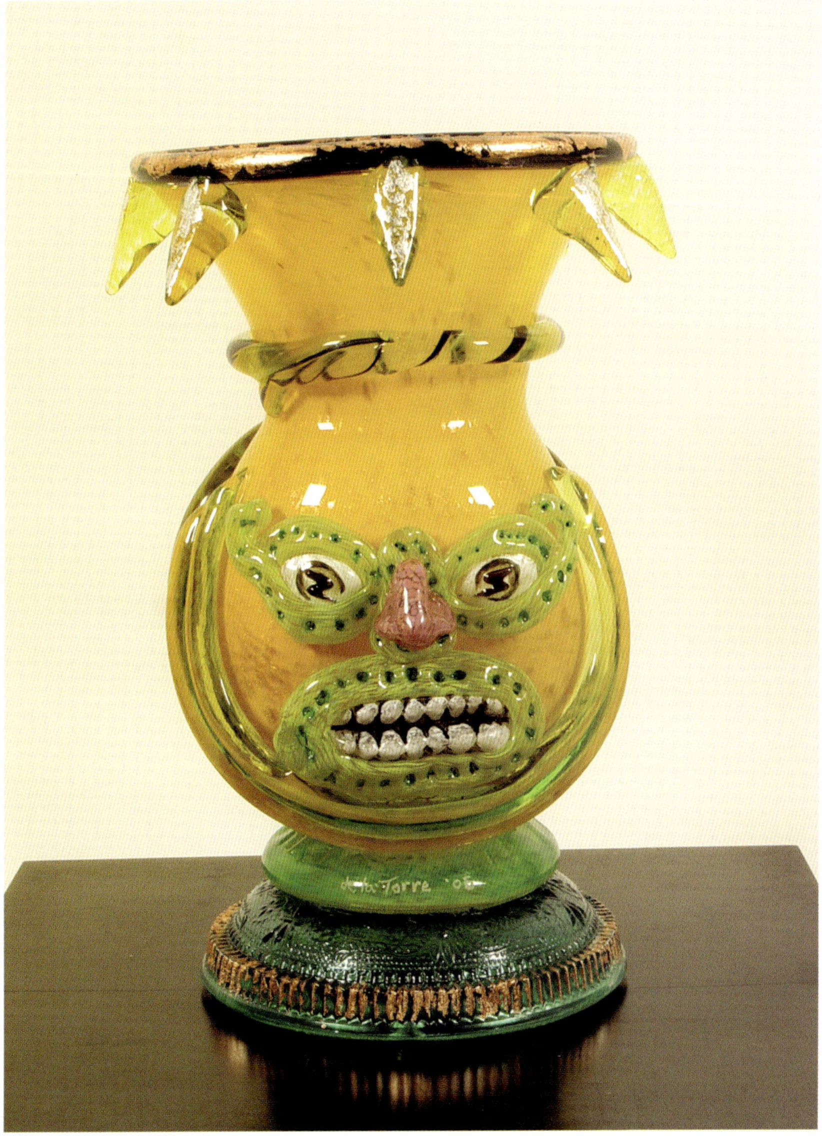

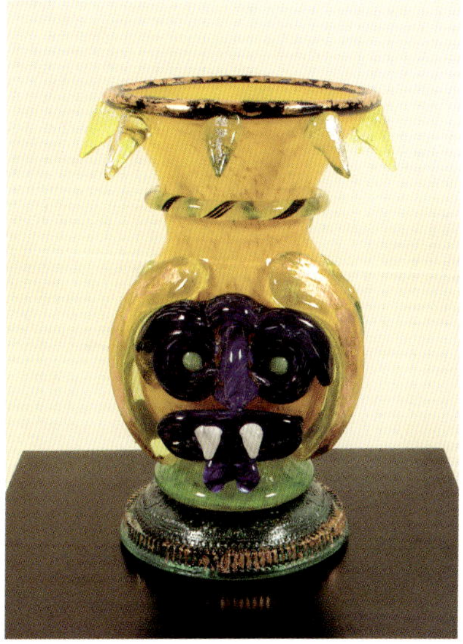

Einar and Jamex collaboration
Tlaloc vs El Rayo, 2005
Mixed media with blown glass
16 x 8 x 9

Those who have crossed boundaries often become fearless. The de la Torre brothers activities and experiences in different territories have enabled them to shatter the common notion of territories, and the common notion of glass too.

Tomoko Aoki, *Glass Document*
exhibition catalog, Kanazu, Japan 1999

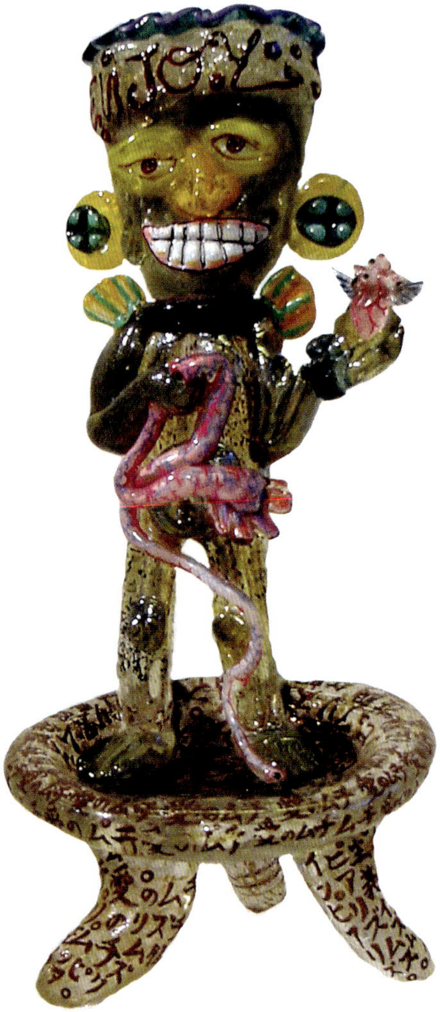

Einar and Jamex collaboration
Ai no Muchi, 1998
Mixed media with blown glass
26 x 11 x 11

Right:
Einar and Jamex collaboration
RuletAzteca, 2004
Mixed media with blown glass
45 x 45 x 11

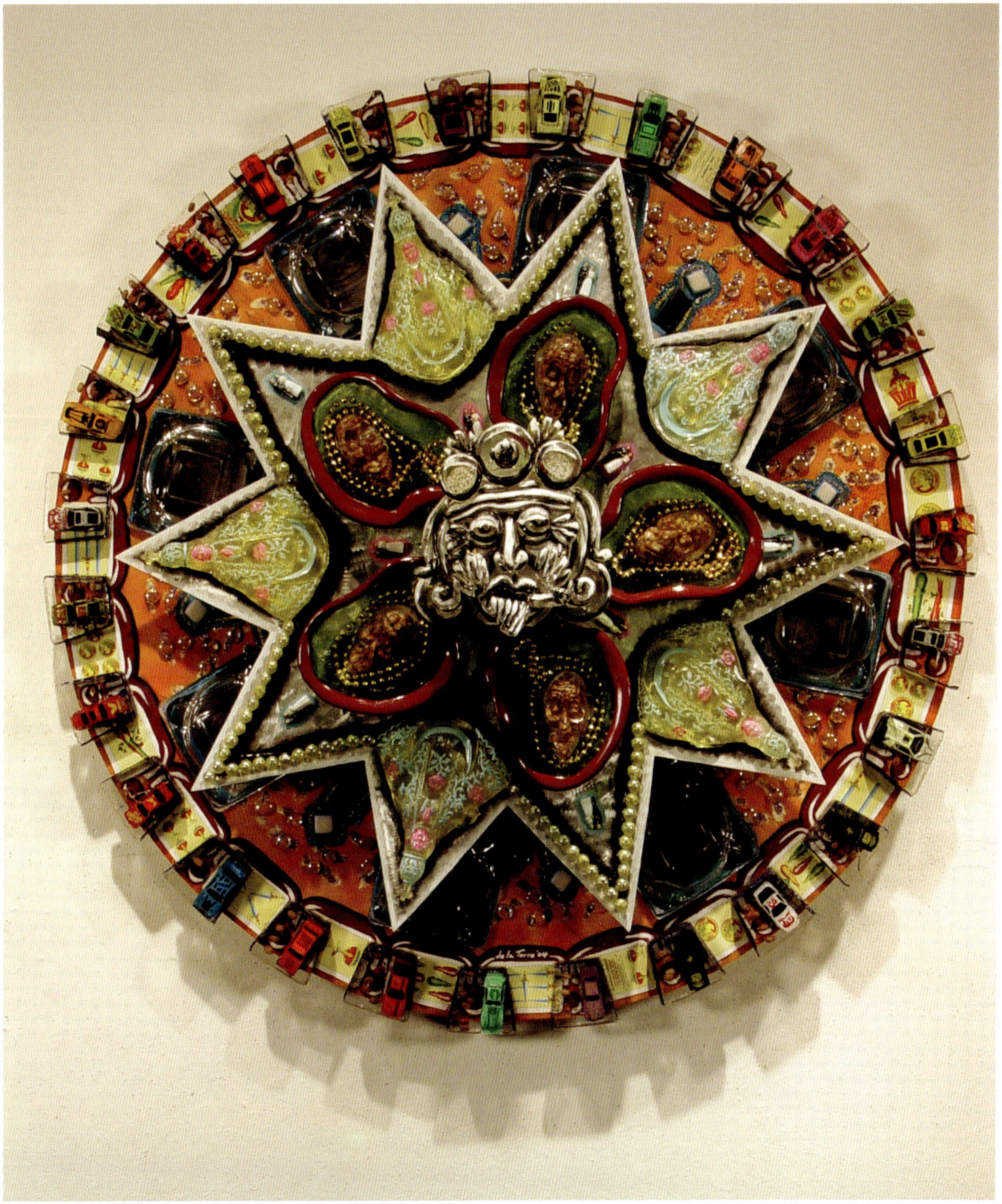

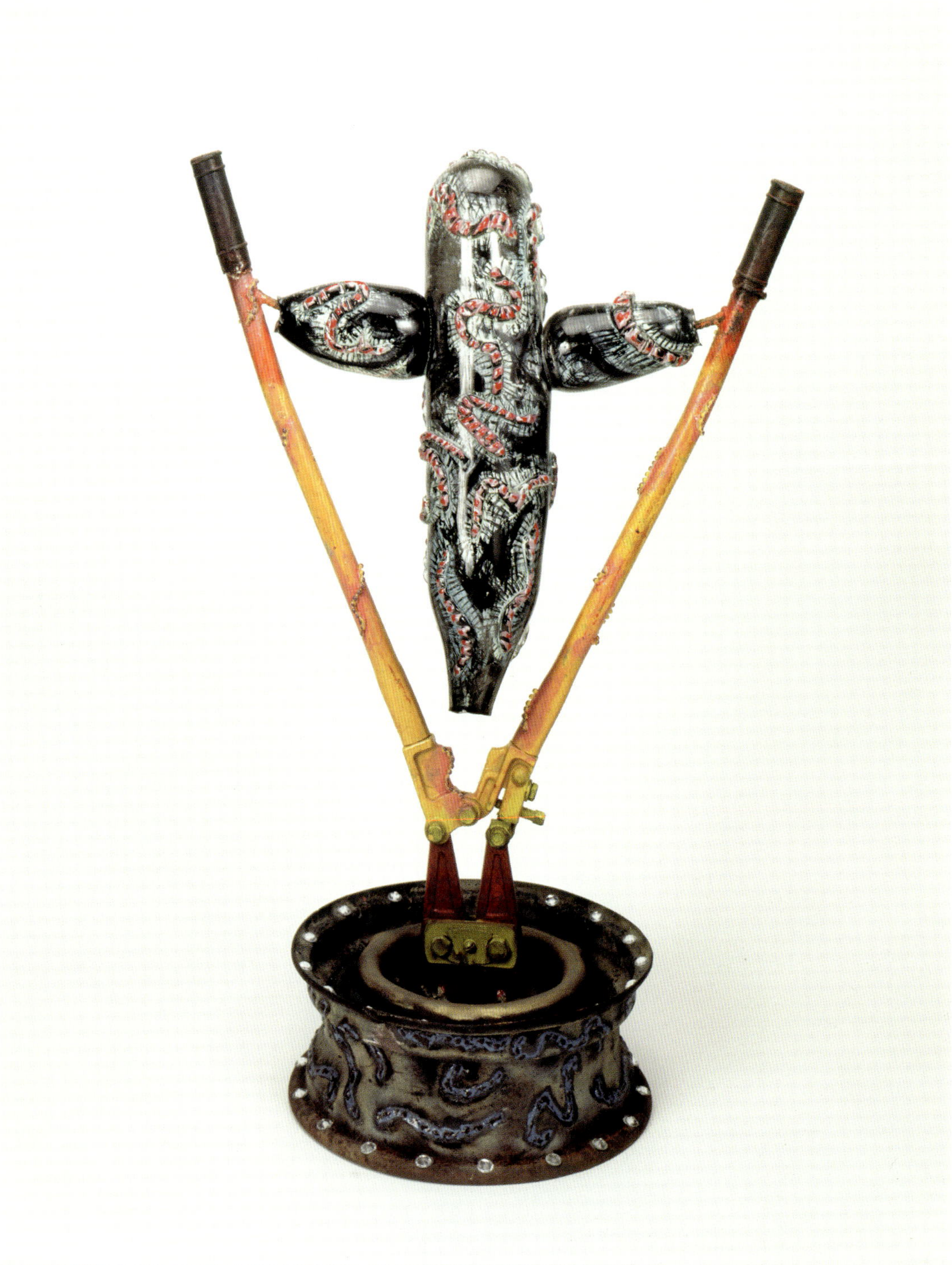

Einar de la Torre
Spiritual Decay, 1995
Mixed media with blown glass
39 x 26 x 16

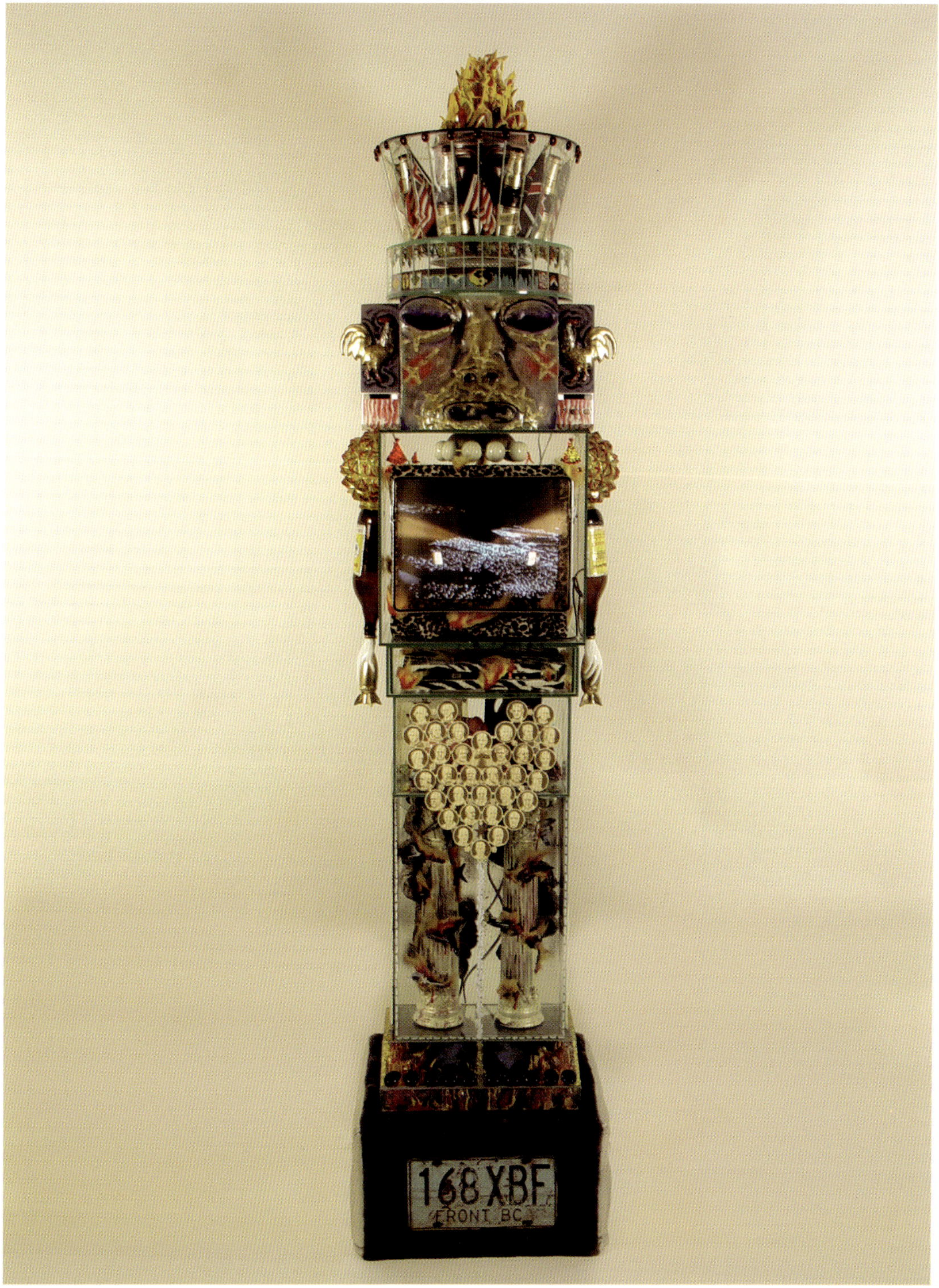

Einar and Jamex collaboration
De Pilar of M. Pyre, 2004
Mixed media with blown glass and video
80 x 24 x 20

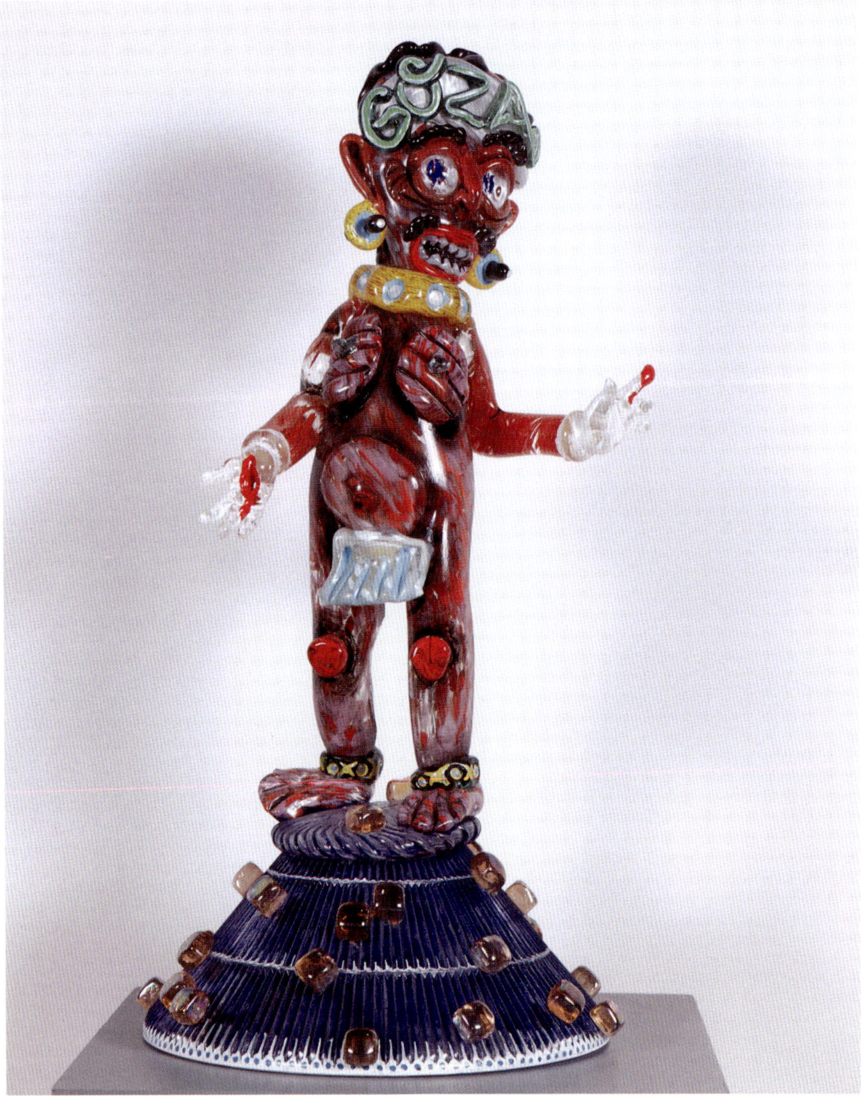

Einar and Jamex collaboration
¡Goza!, 2001
30 x 16 x 16
Collection of George and Lynn Goldstein, Santa Fe, NM

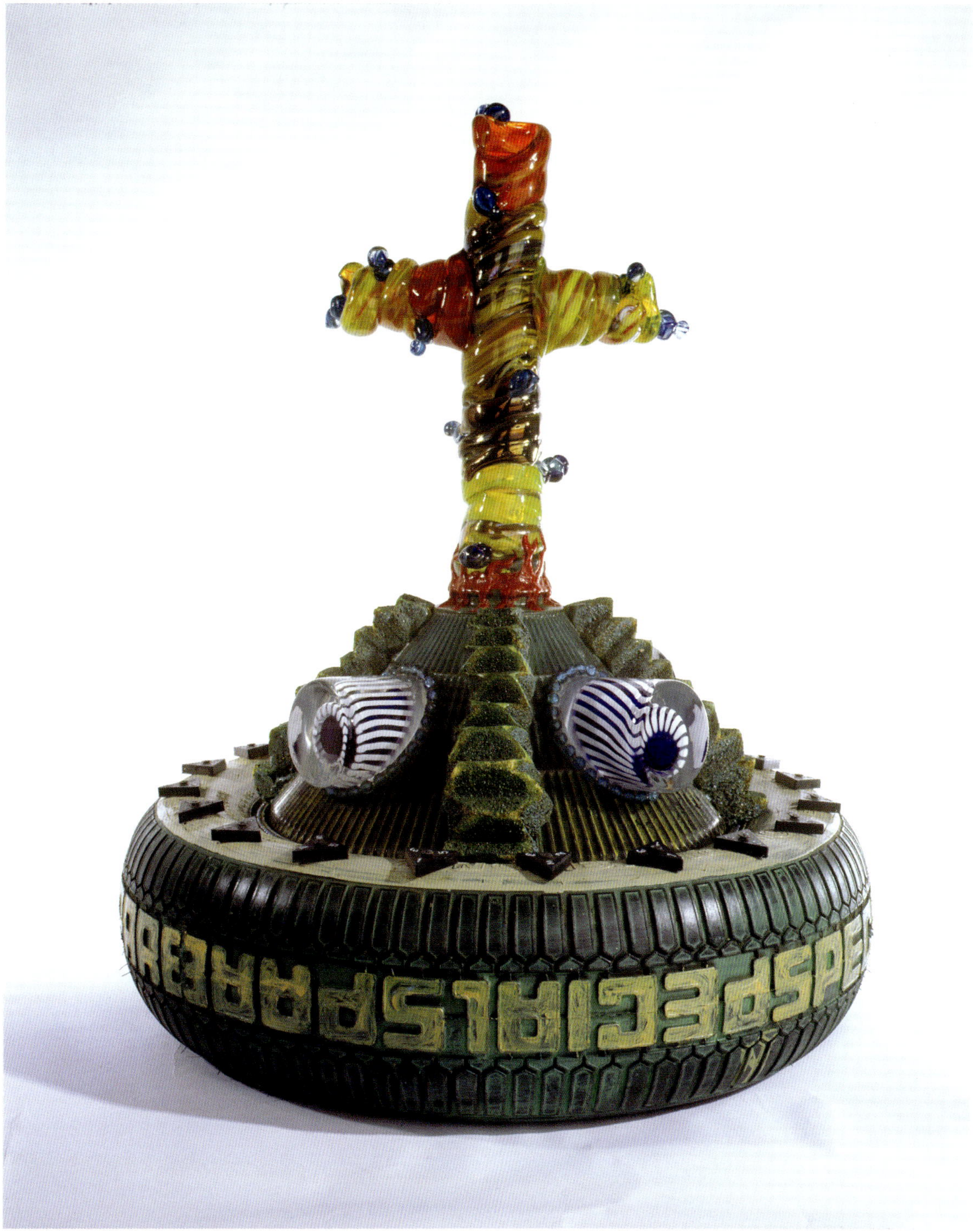

Einar de la Torre
Special Spare, 1997
Mixed media with blown glass
28 x 24 x 24

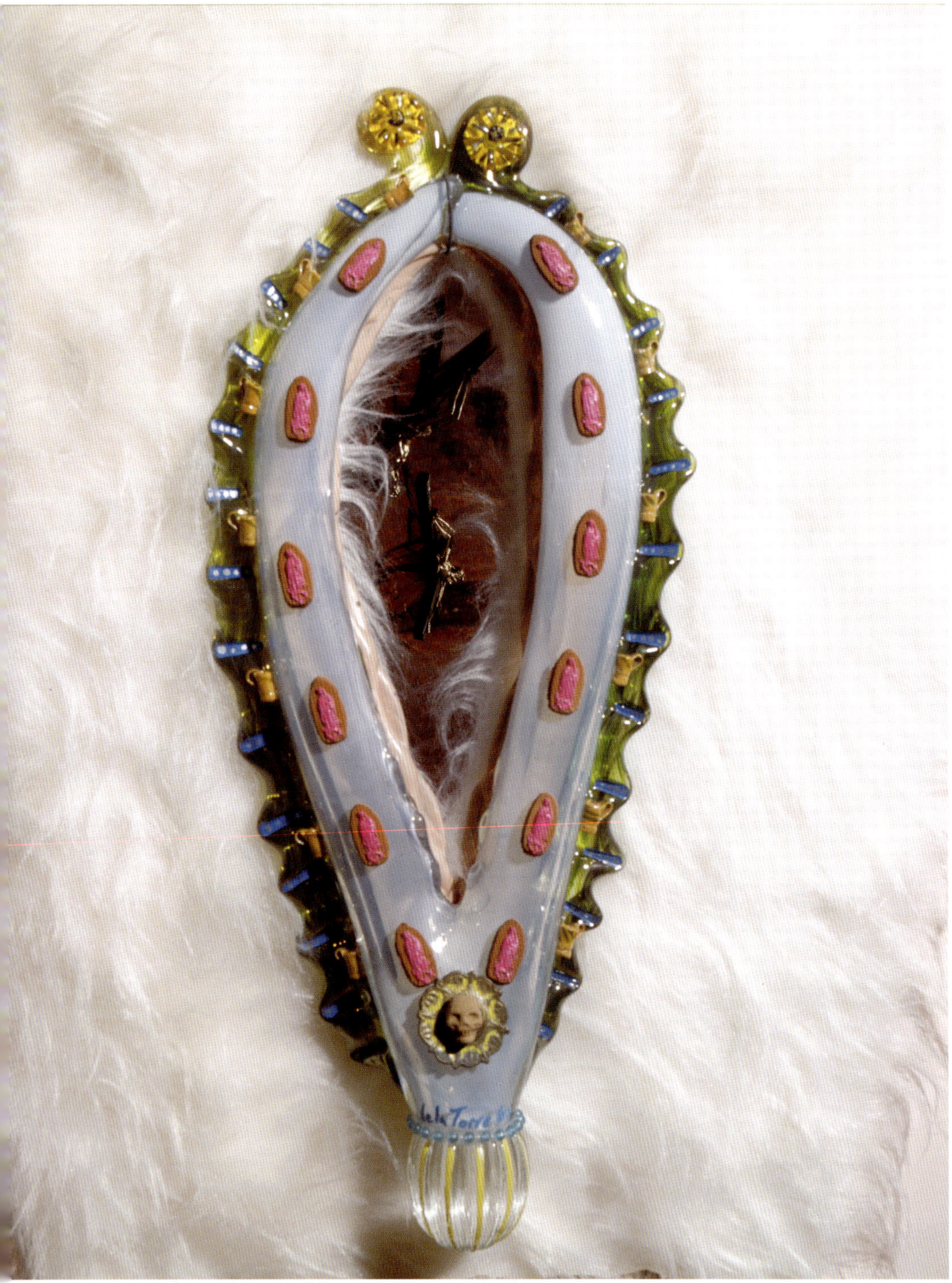

Einar and Jamex collaboration
Virgen Vagina Series
Detail from installation
El Valle de las Monarcas, 2002
Mixed media with blown glass
Varied dimensions
Museo de la Artes, Guadalajara, Mexico

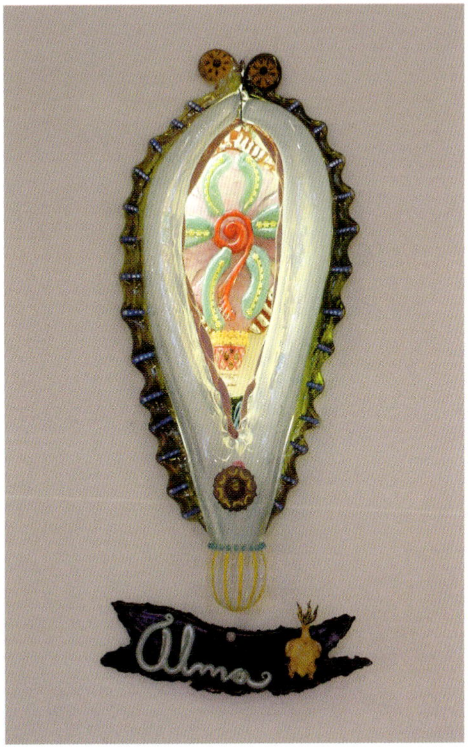

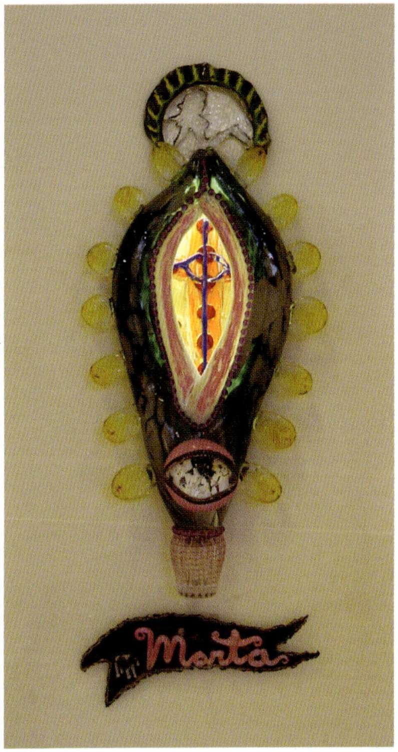

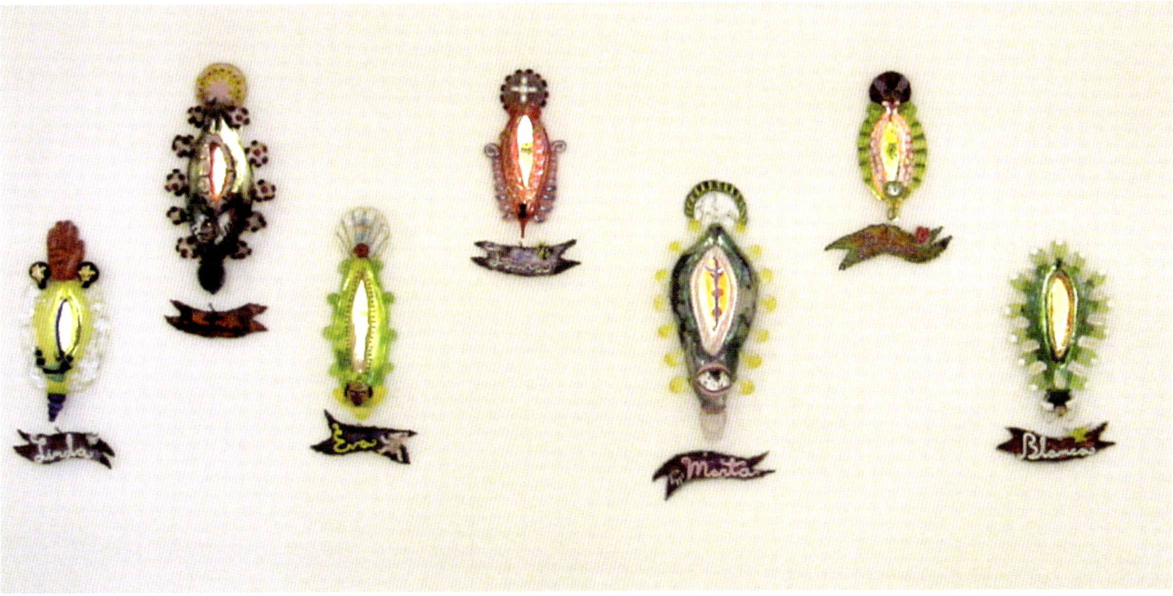

Einar and Jamex collaboration
Virgen Vagina Series
Alma and Marta, 2001
Mixed media with blown glass
Varied dimensions

Virgen Vagina Series
Installation, 2001
Mixed media with blown glass

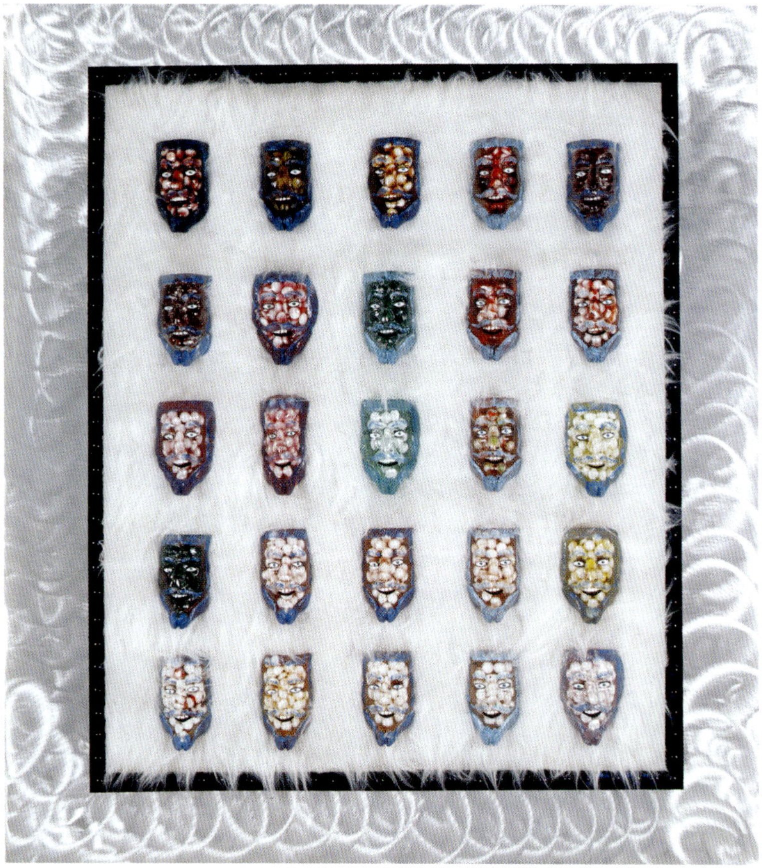

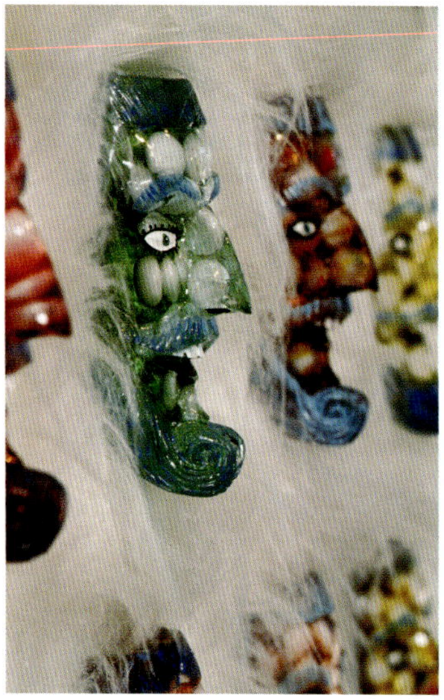

Einar and Jamex collaboration
Eurovirus, 2001
Mixed media with cast glass
48 x 54 x 6
Collection of Margaret and Quincy Troupe, New York, NY

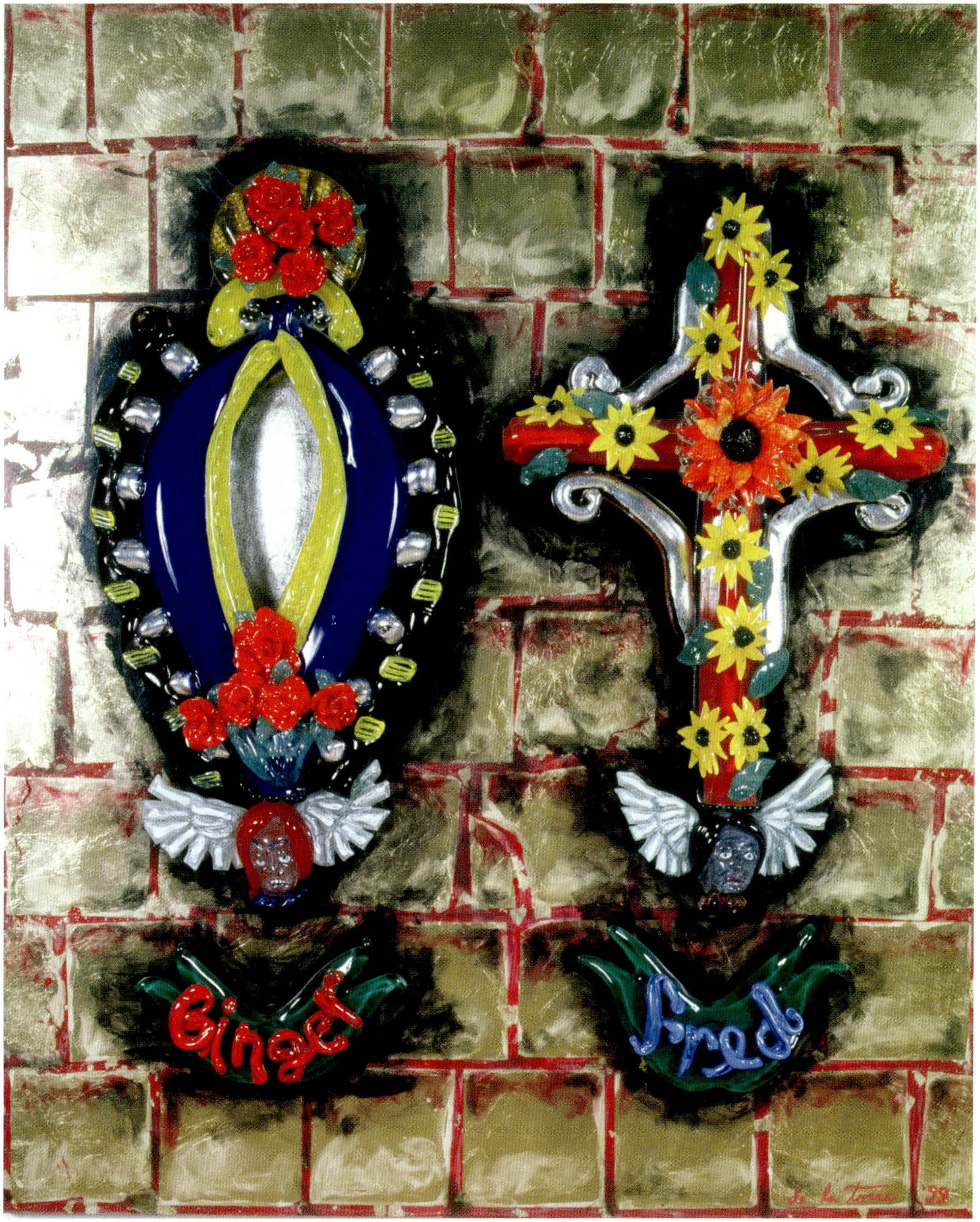

Einar and Jamex collaboration
Ginger and Fred, 1999
Mixed media with blown glass
48 x 40 x 6

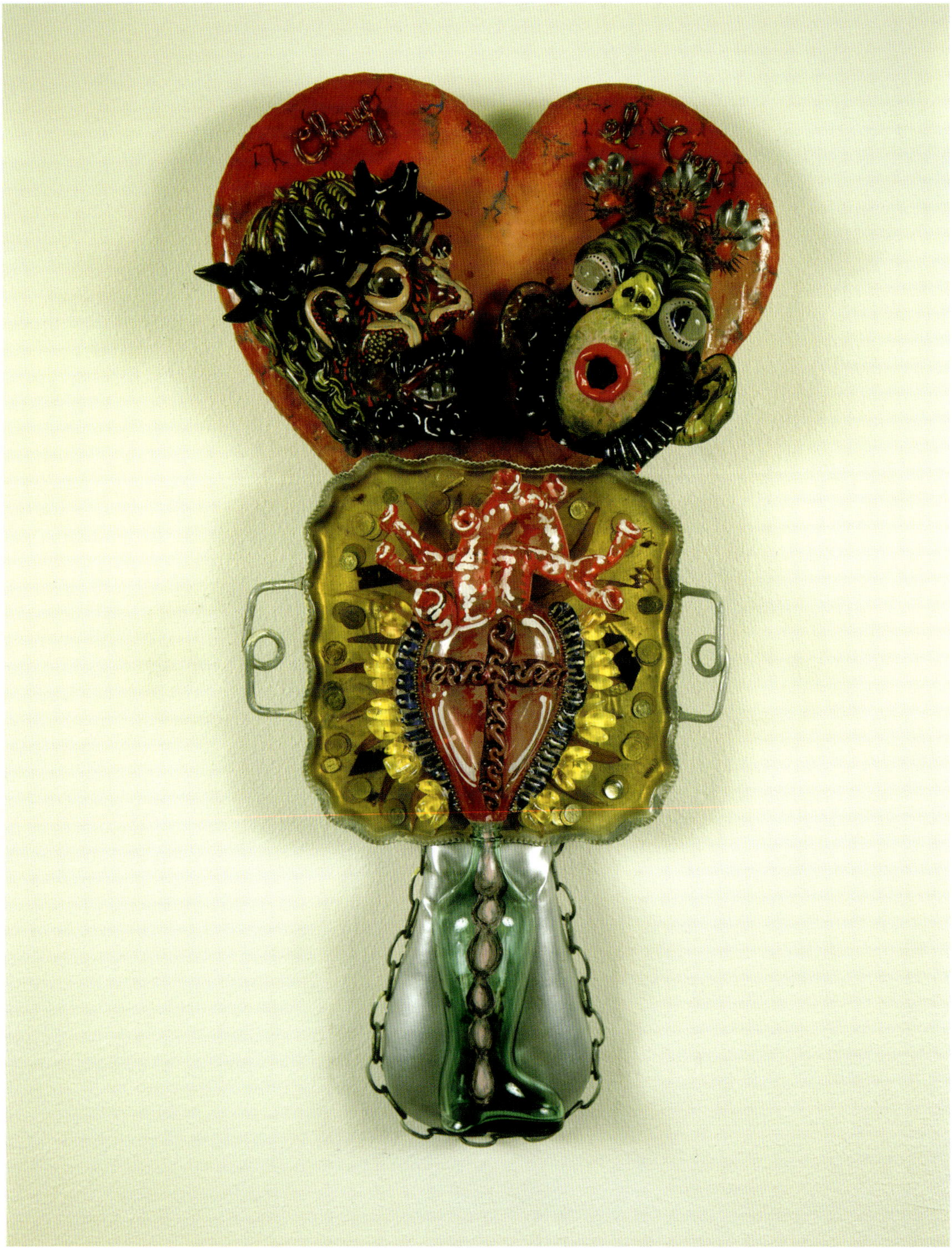

Jamex de la Torre
Chuy y el Cien, 1999
Mixed media with blown glass
40 x 22 x 9

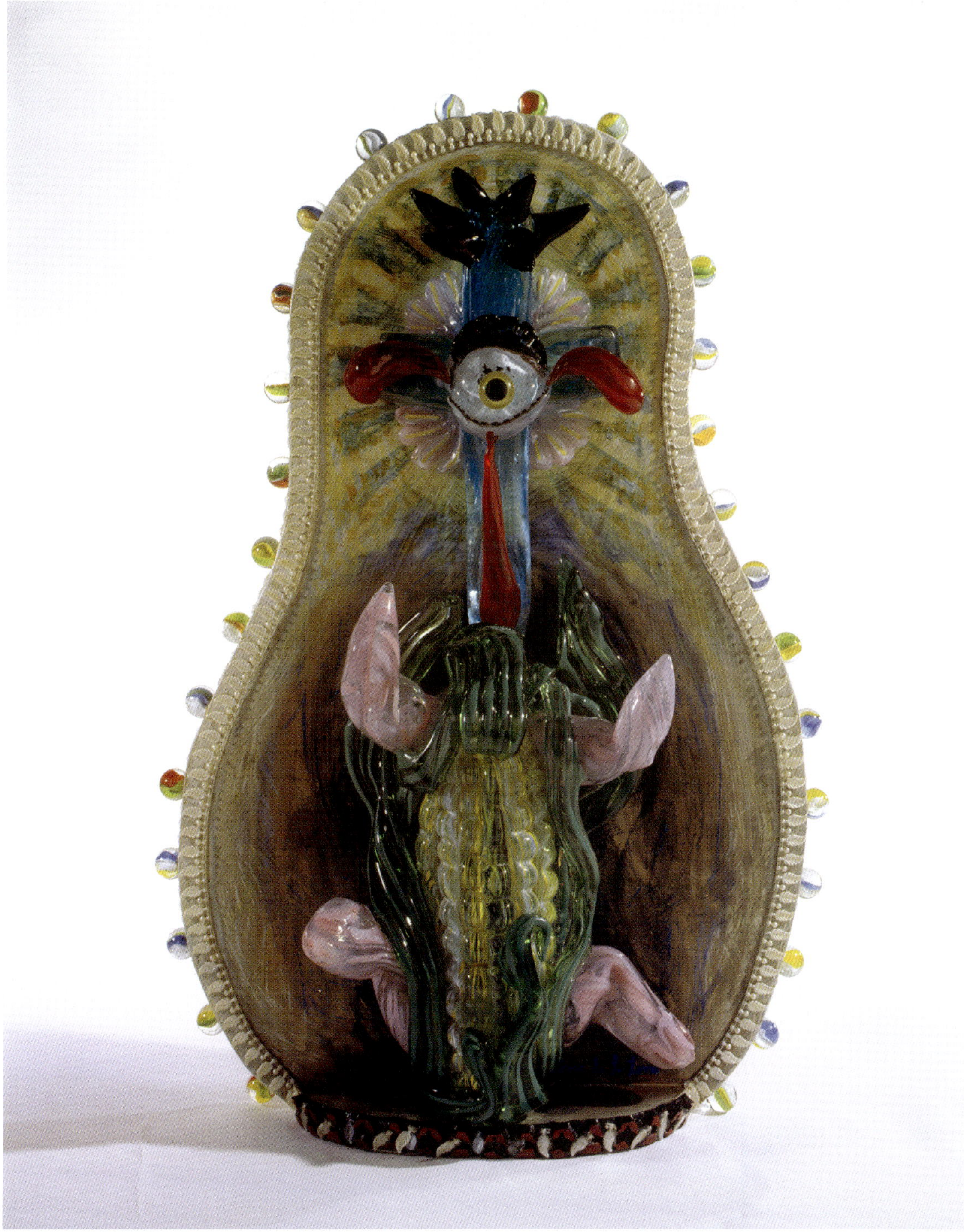

Einar de la Torre
Corn Baby, 1997
Mixed media with blown glass
28 x 18 x 7

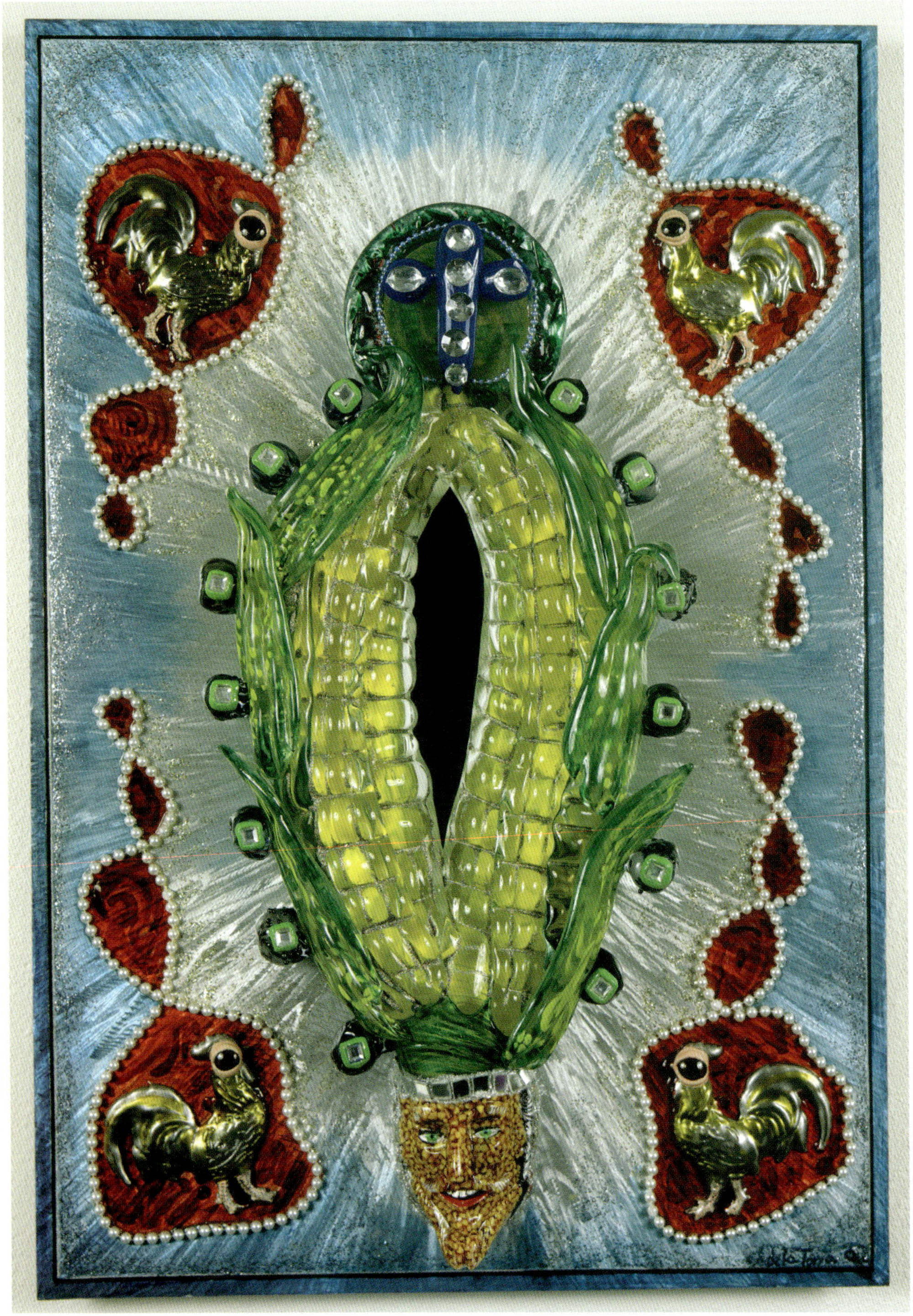

Einar and Jamex collaboration
Pecking Order, 2002
Mixed media with blown glass
36 x 25 x 6

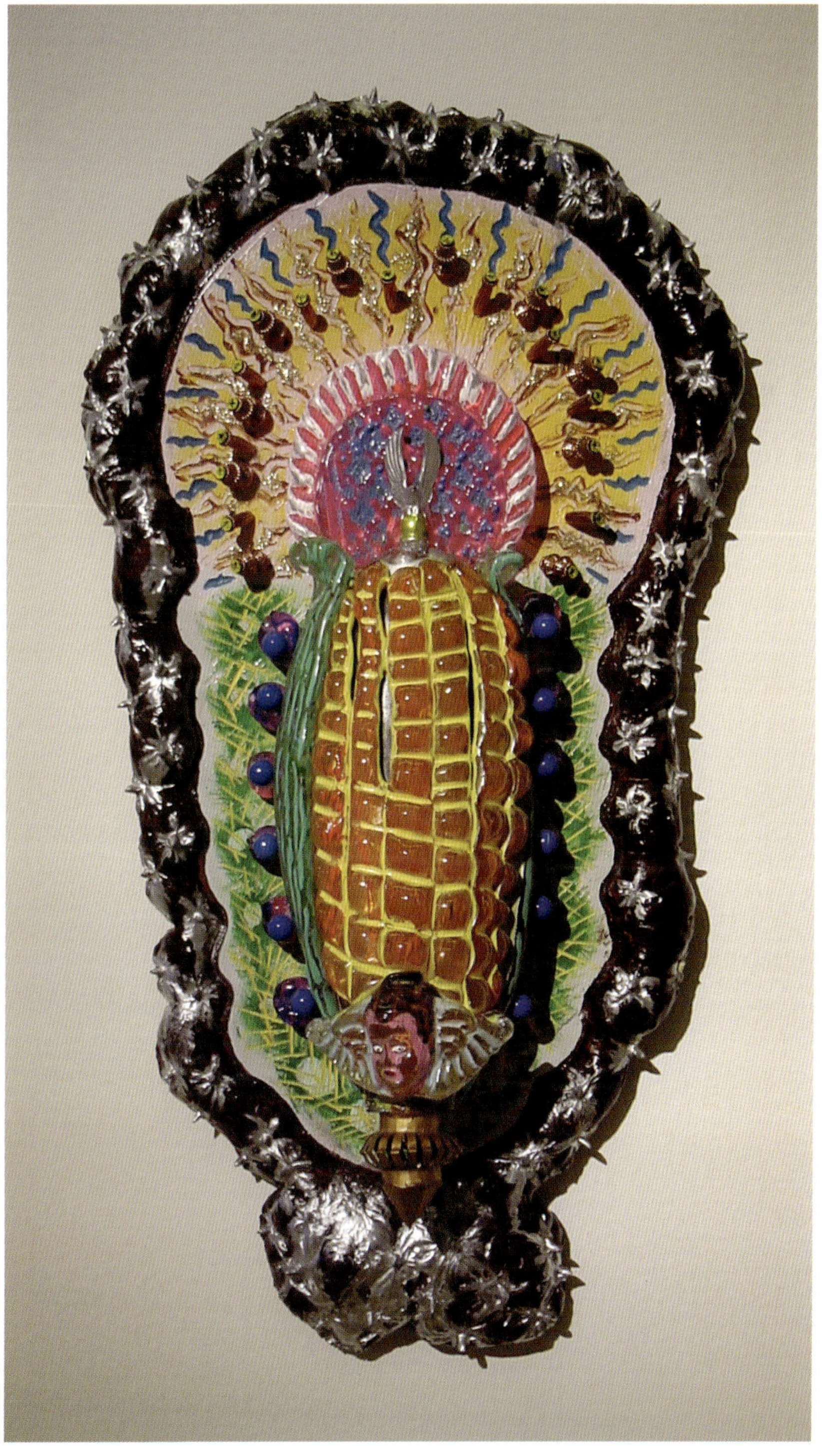

Einar de la Torre
Virgen Elotera, 1997
Mixed media with blown glass
35 x 25 x 10

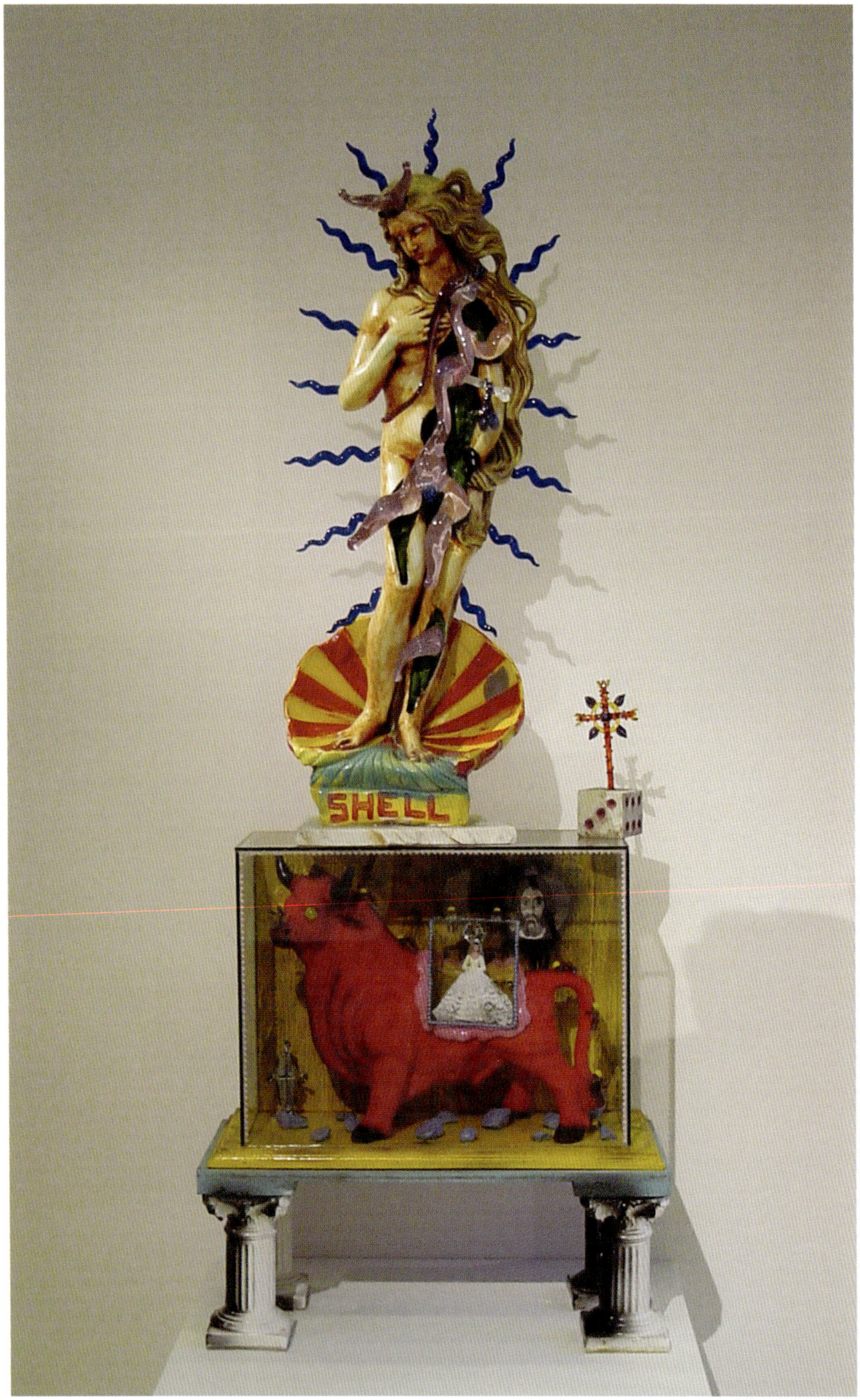

Einar and Jamex collaboration
Marte y Venus, 1997
Mixed media
62 x 25 x 12
Collection of Sandy Besser, Santa Fe, NM

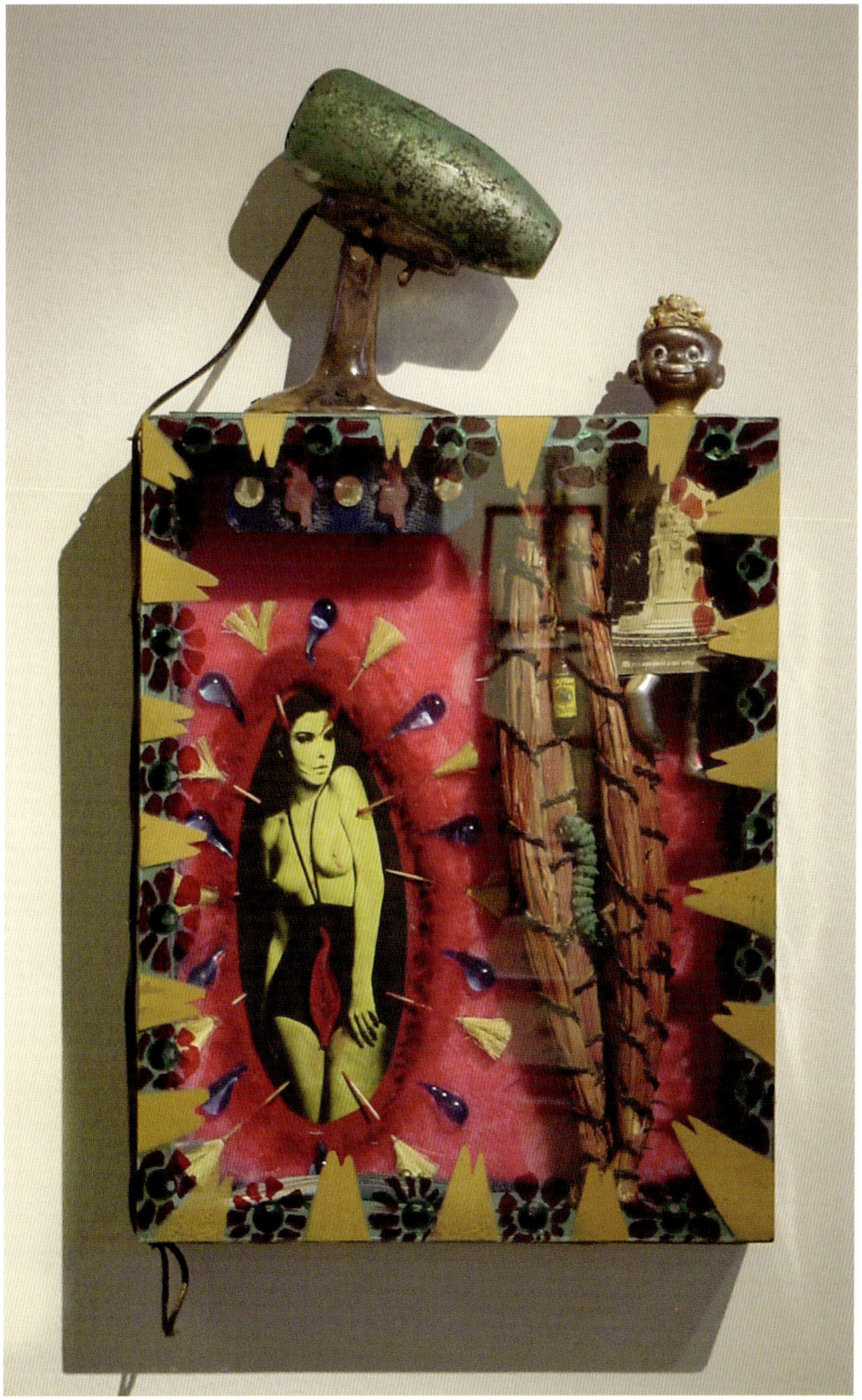

Einar de la Torre
Popcorn, 1996
Mixed media
28 x 17 x 5

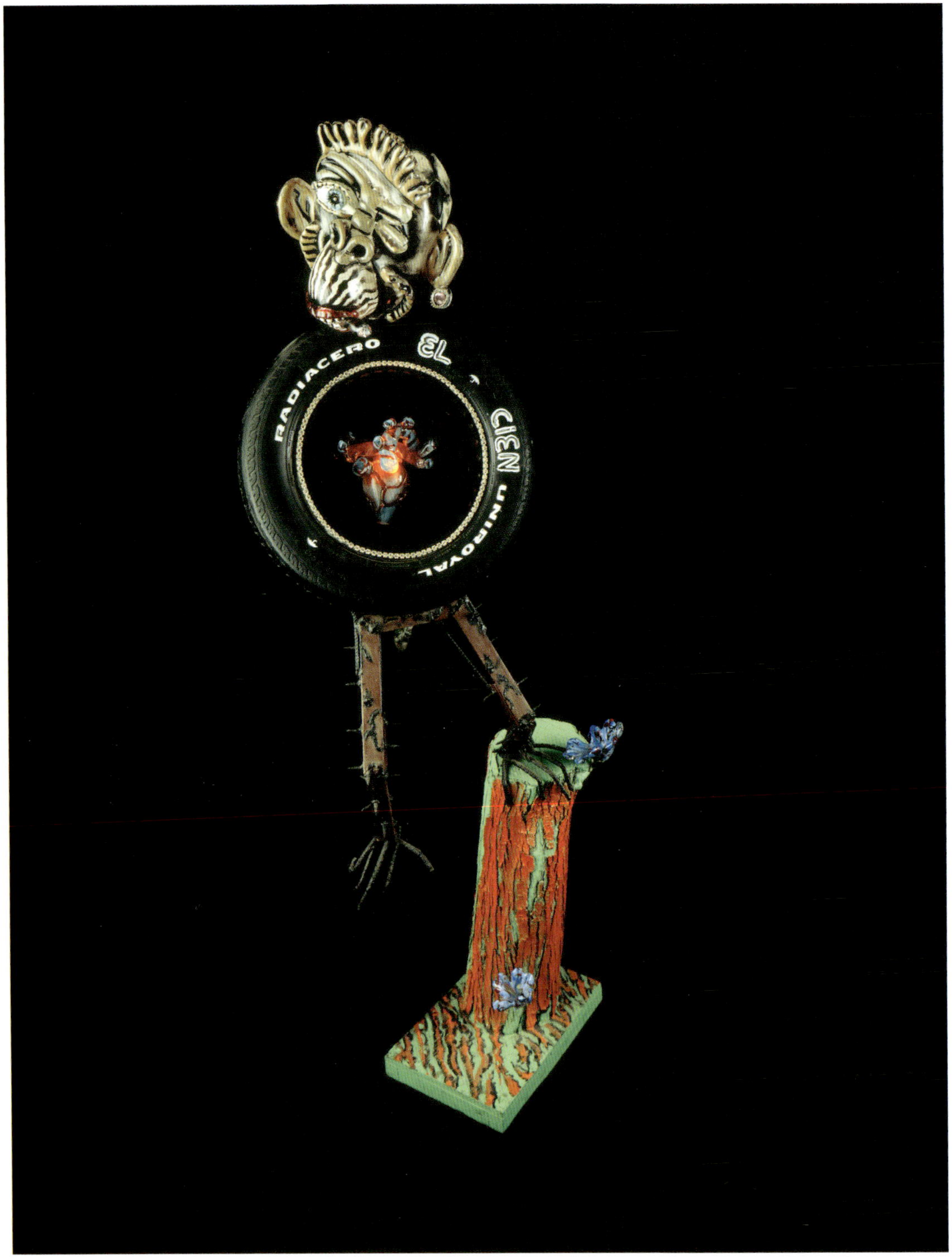

Einar and Jamex collaboration
El Cien, 1997
Mixed media with blown glass
74 x 30 x 15

Right:
Acido Folclorico, 2000
Installation
Centro Cultural de Tijuana, Tijuana, México
Curated by Olga Margarita Dávila

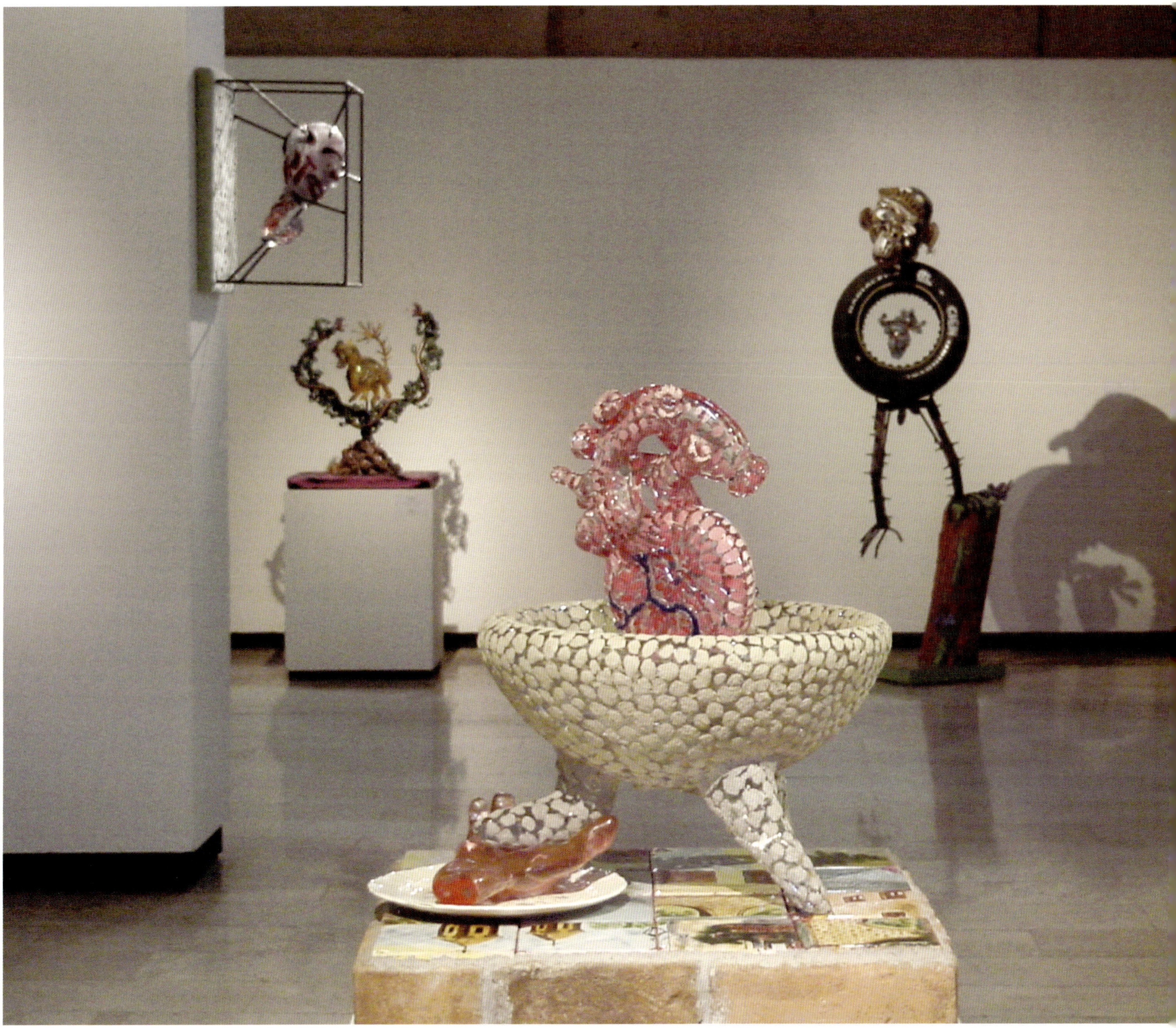

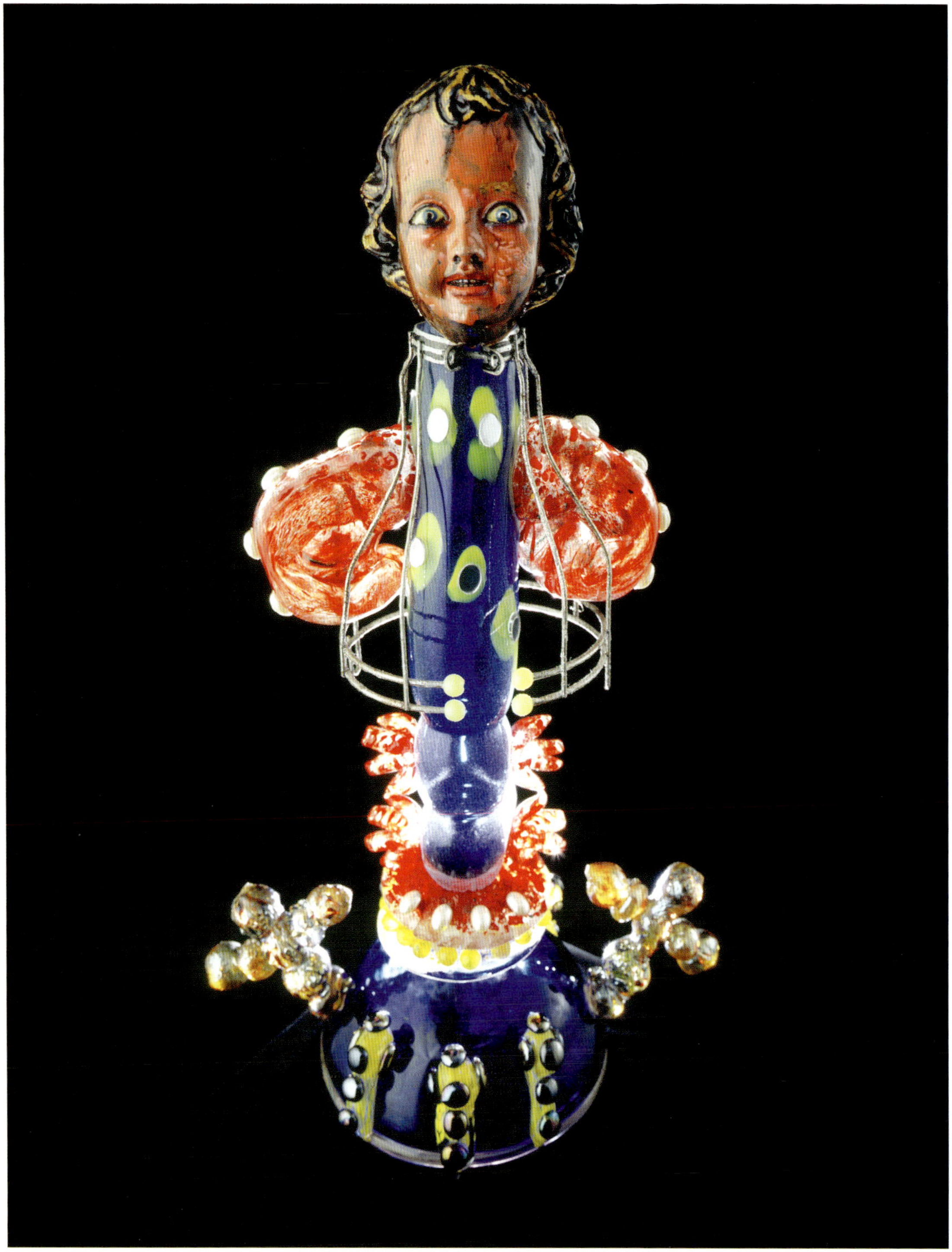

Einar de la Torre
El Blue Boy, 1998
Mixed media with blown glass
26 x 15 x 10

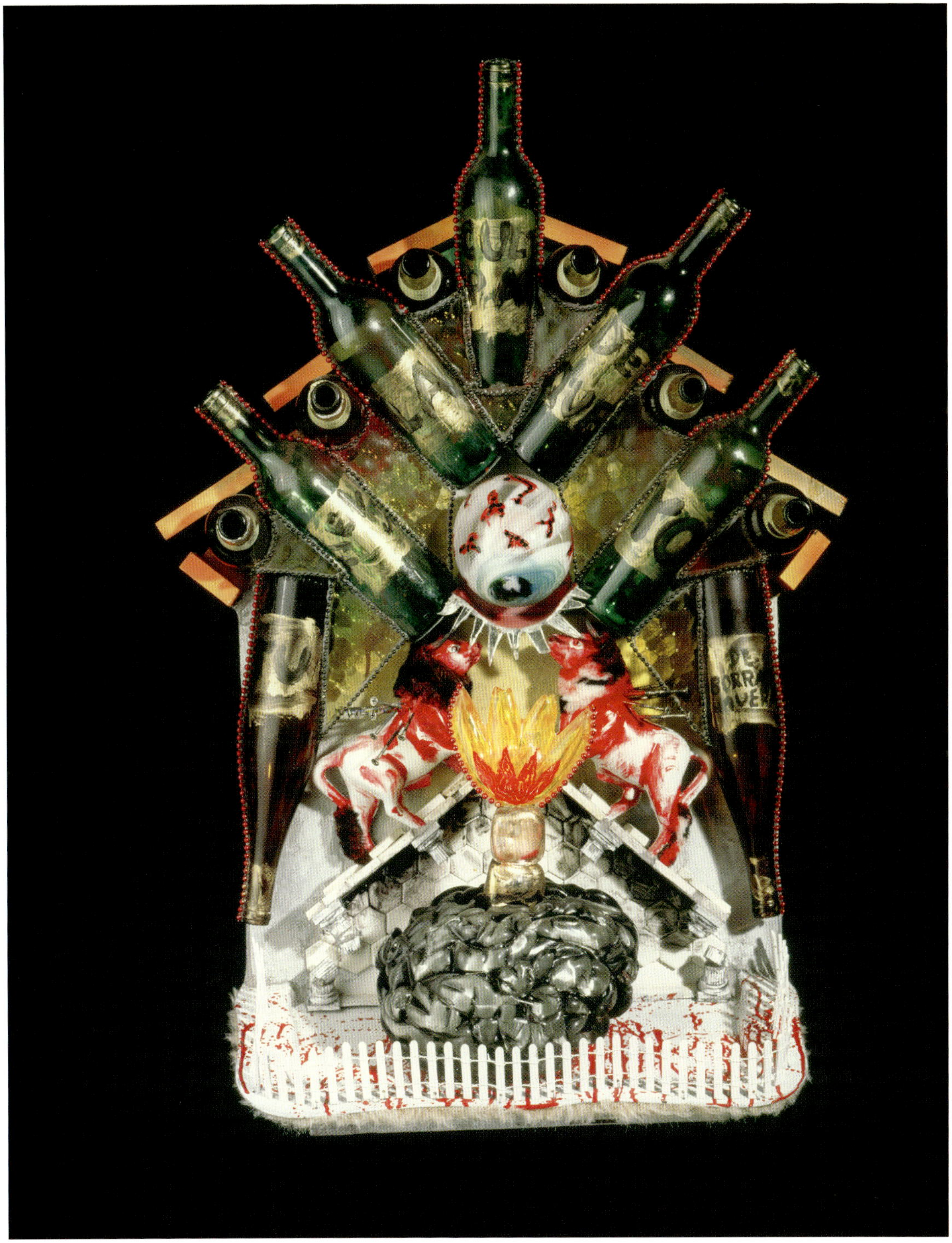

Jamex de la Torre
Visionary Flood of the Alcohol, 1995
Mixed media with blown glass
37 x 27 x 10

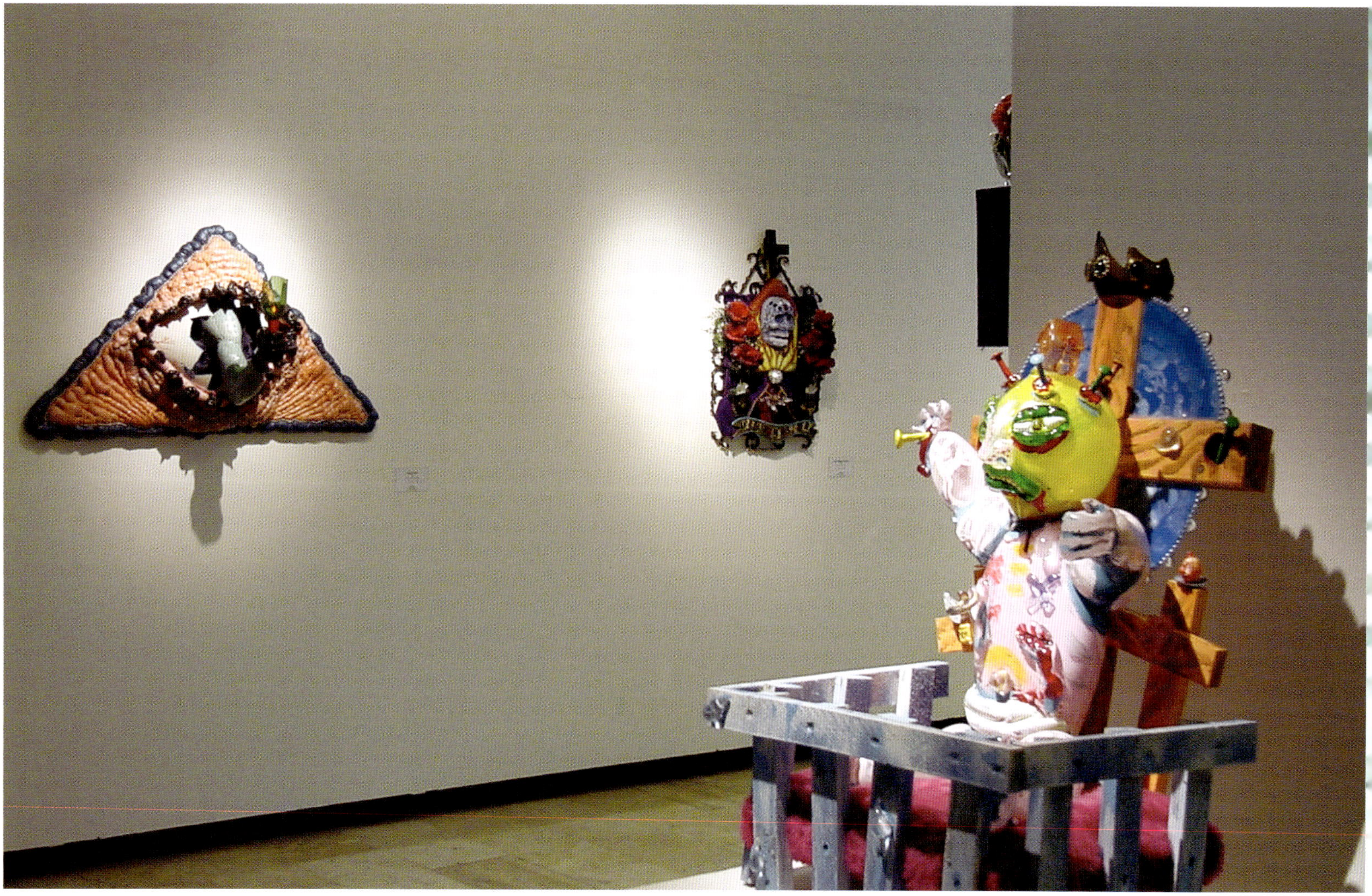

"…….the attempt is not anachronistic so much as quixotic. The de la Torre brothers are having a good time and making great art, allowing us in on the jokes and violence and irony and frustration of living in post-everything world."

Marilyn A. Zeitlin, Phoienix, AZ, for the exhibition catalog,
MexicArte Museum Austin, TX, 2001

Acido Folclorico, 2000
Installation
Centro Cultural de Tijuana, Tijuana, México
Curated by Olga Margarita Dávila

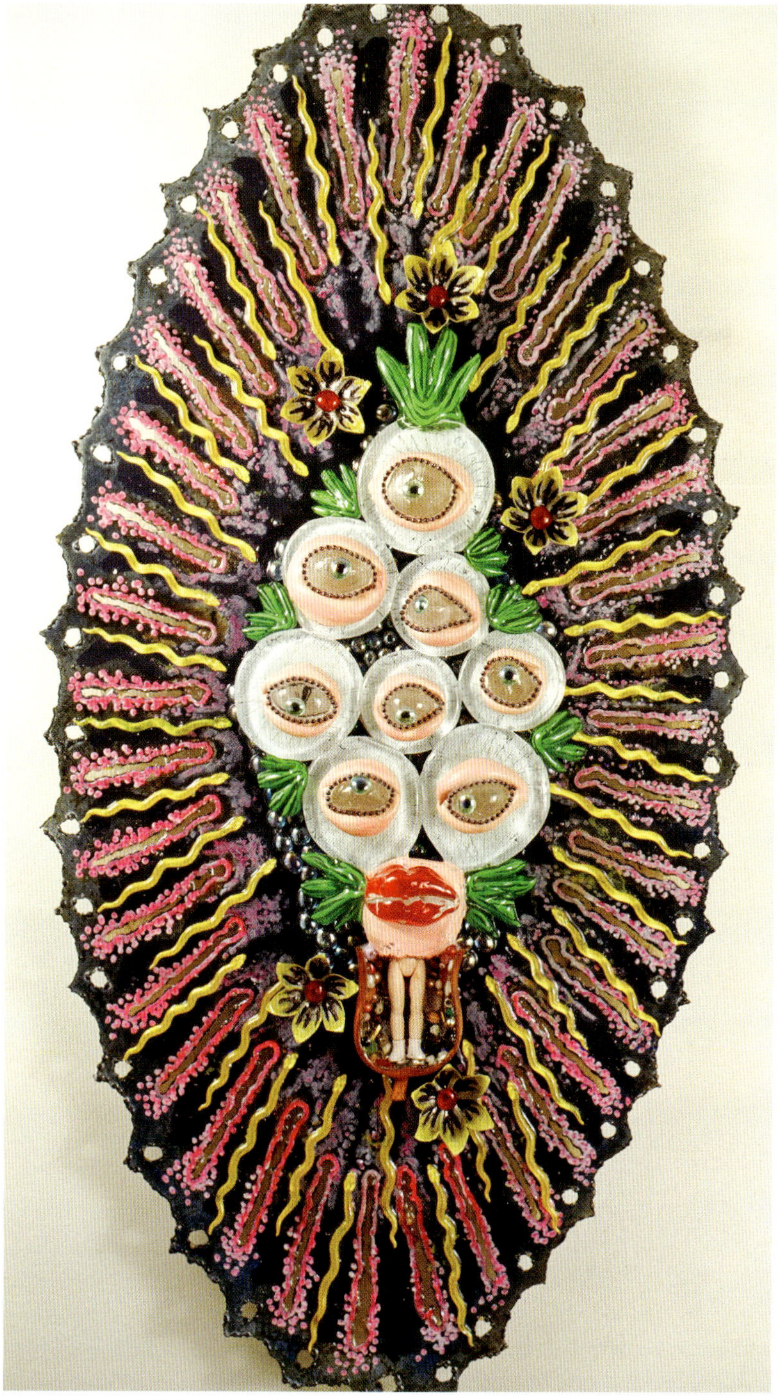

Einar and Jamex collaboration
Mitosis Fronterizo, 1999
Mixed media with blown glass
48 x 24 x 5
Collection of Lucy Goldman, San Diego, CA

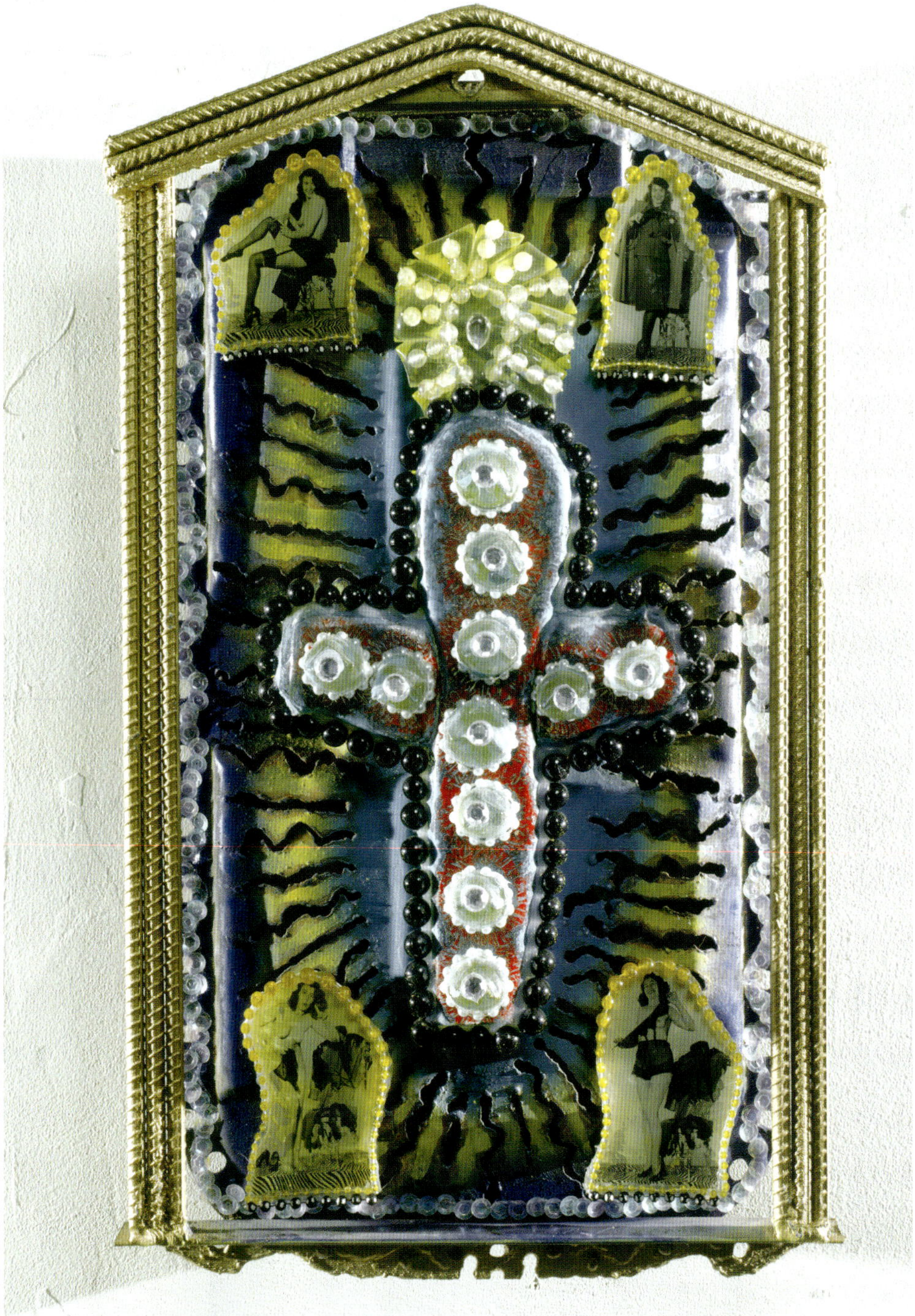

Einar and Jamex collaboration
Sinners Lounge, 1995
Mixed media with blown glass
26 x 15 x 5

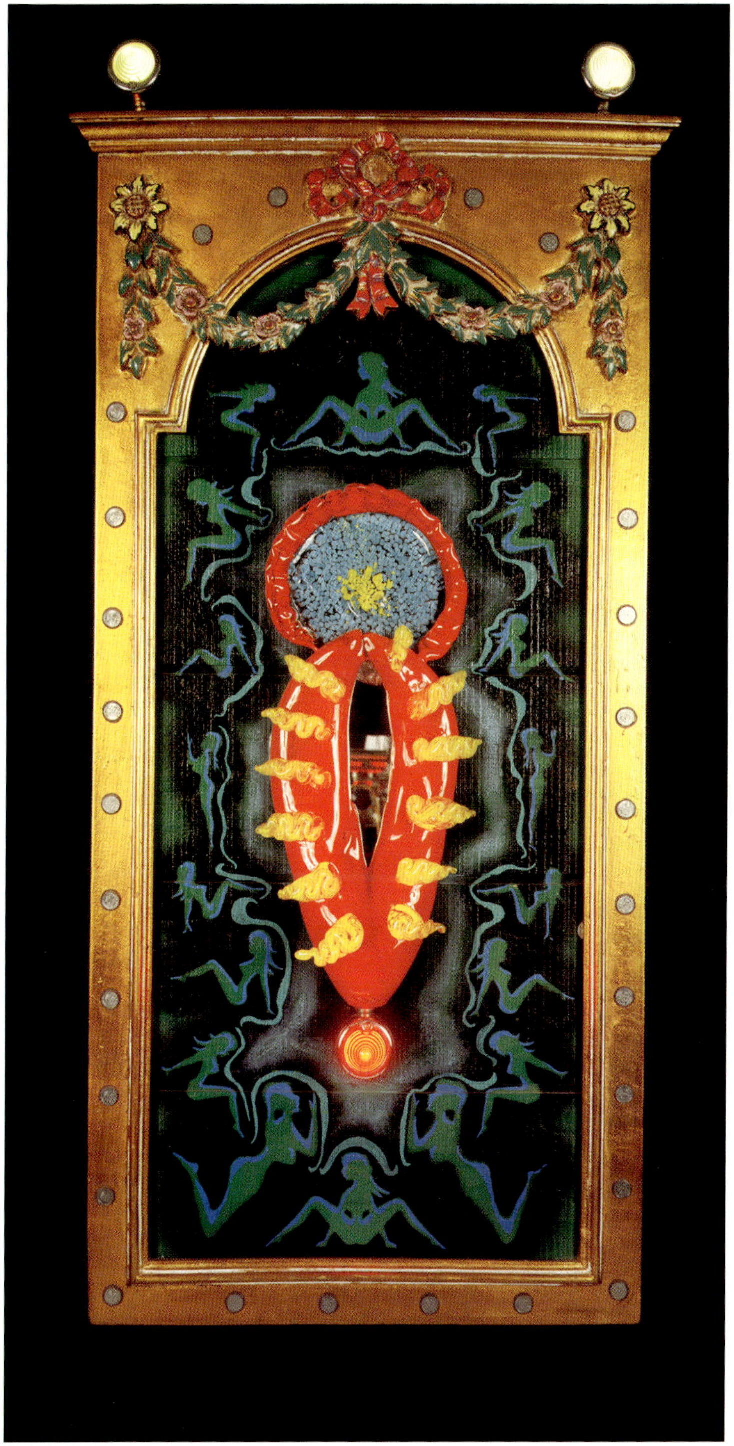

Einar de la Torre
Soy Virgen, 1997
Mixed media with blown glass
48 x 24 x 6

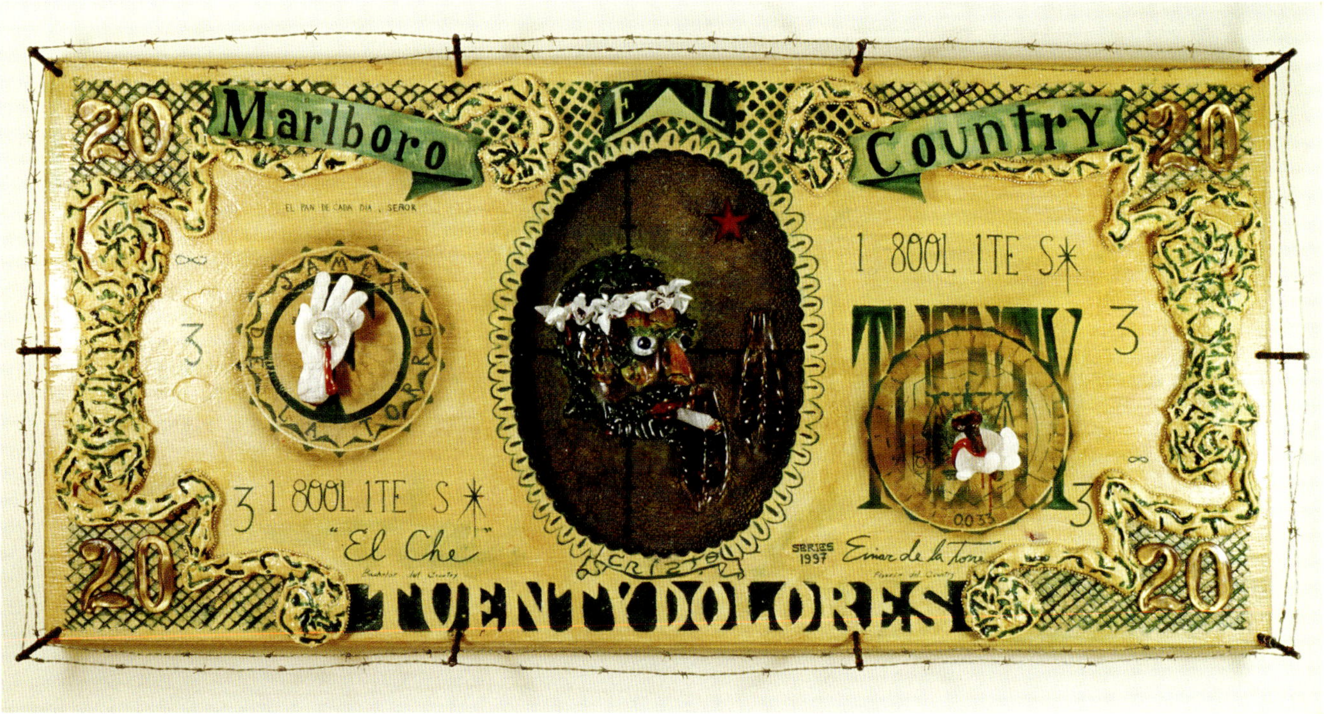

Einar and Jamex collaboration
El Country, 1997
Mixed media with blown glass
38 x 80 x 13
Collection of Stanley and Mikki Weithorn, Scottsdale, AZ

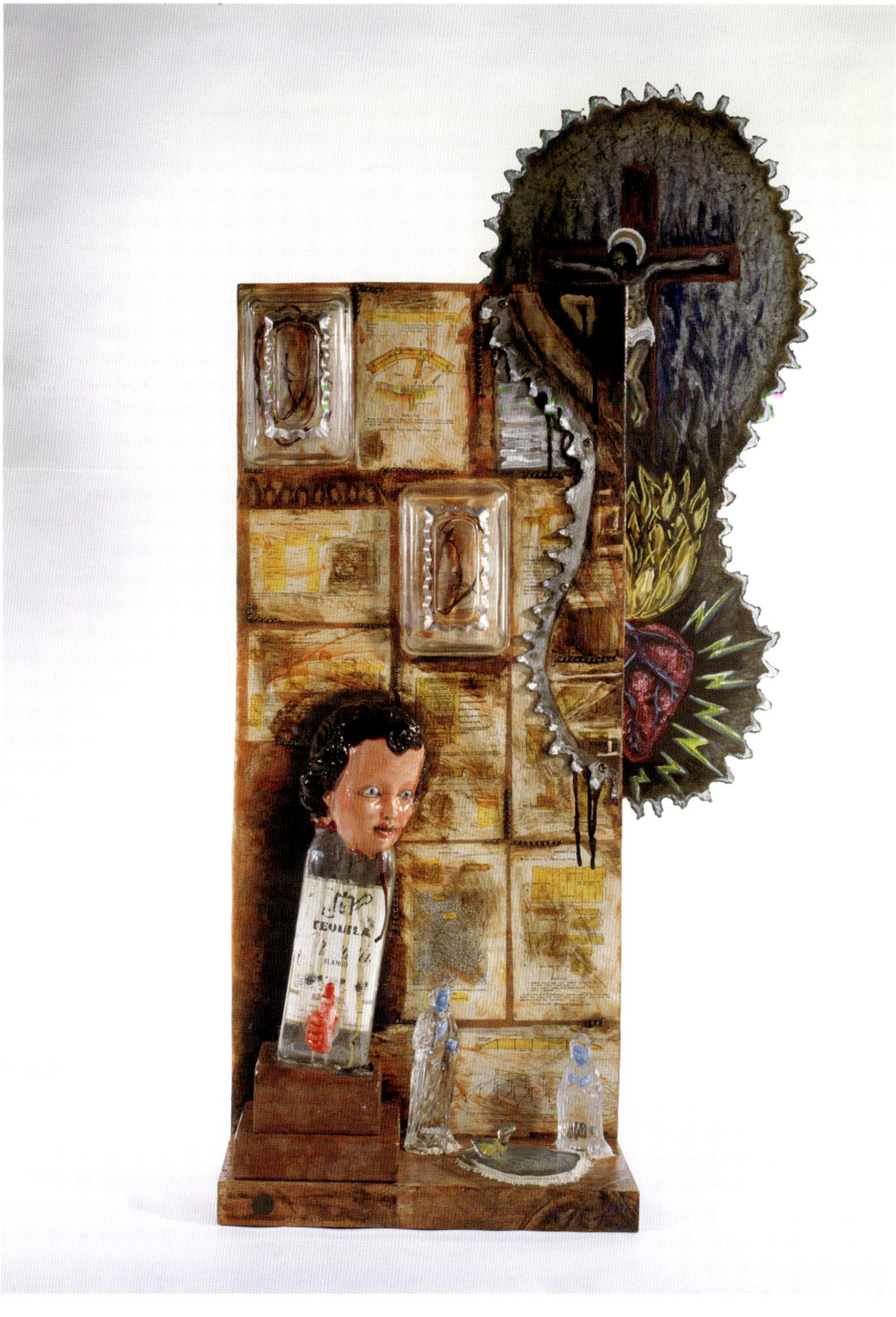

Einar and Jamex collaboration
Los Ingenieros del Apocalipsis, 1999
Mixed media
44 x 22 x 9
Private Collection

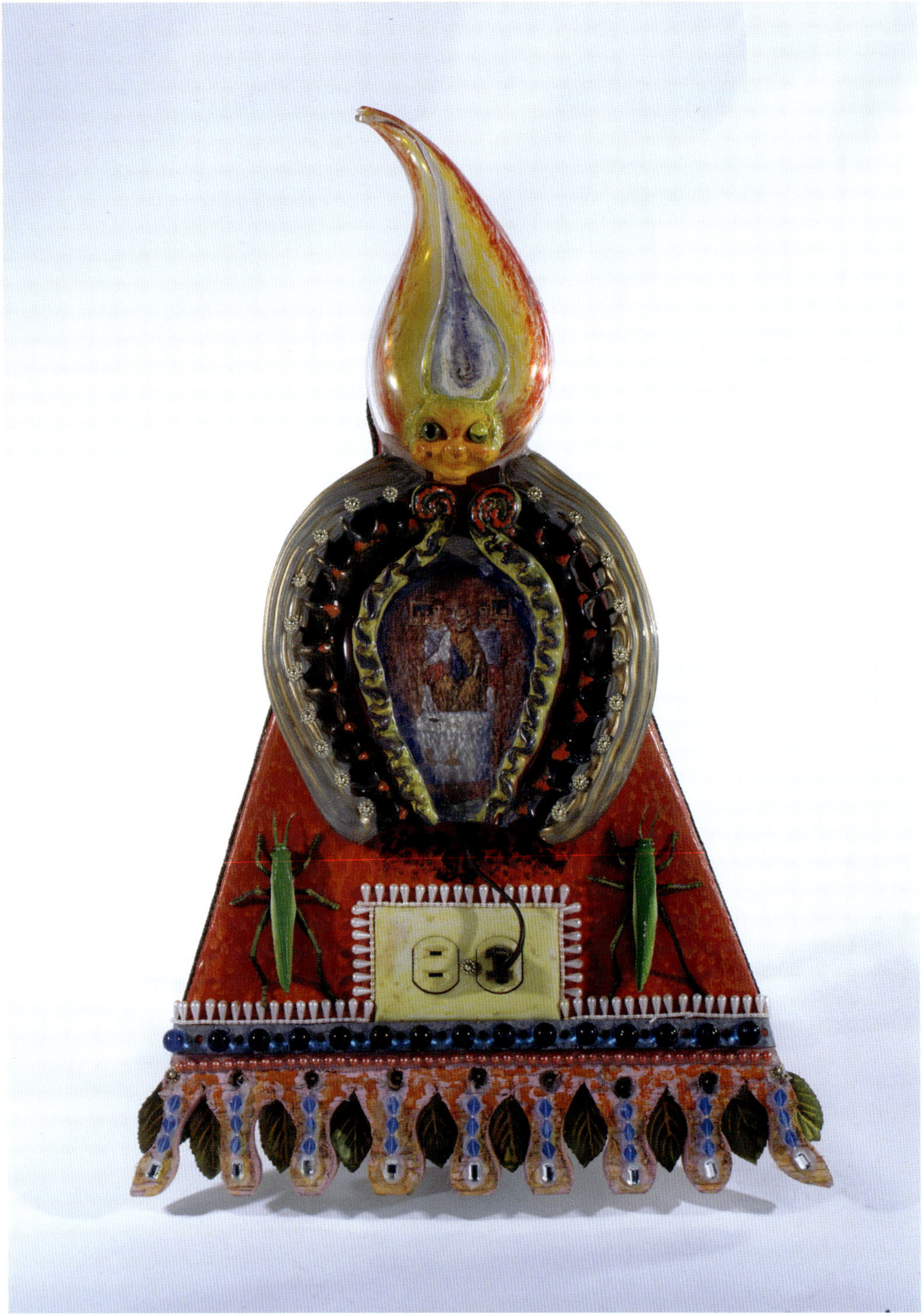

Einar de la Torre
Nomas Enchufala, 1995
Mixed media with blown glass
26 x 17 x 4

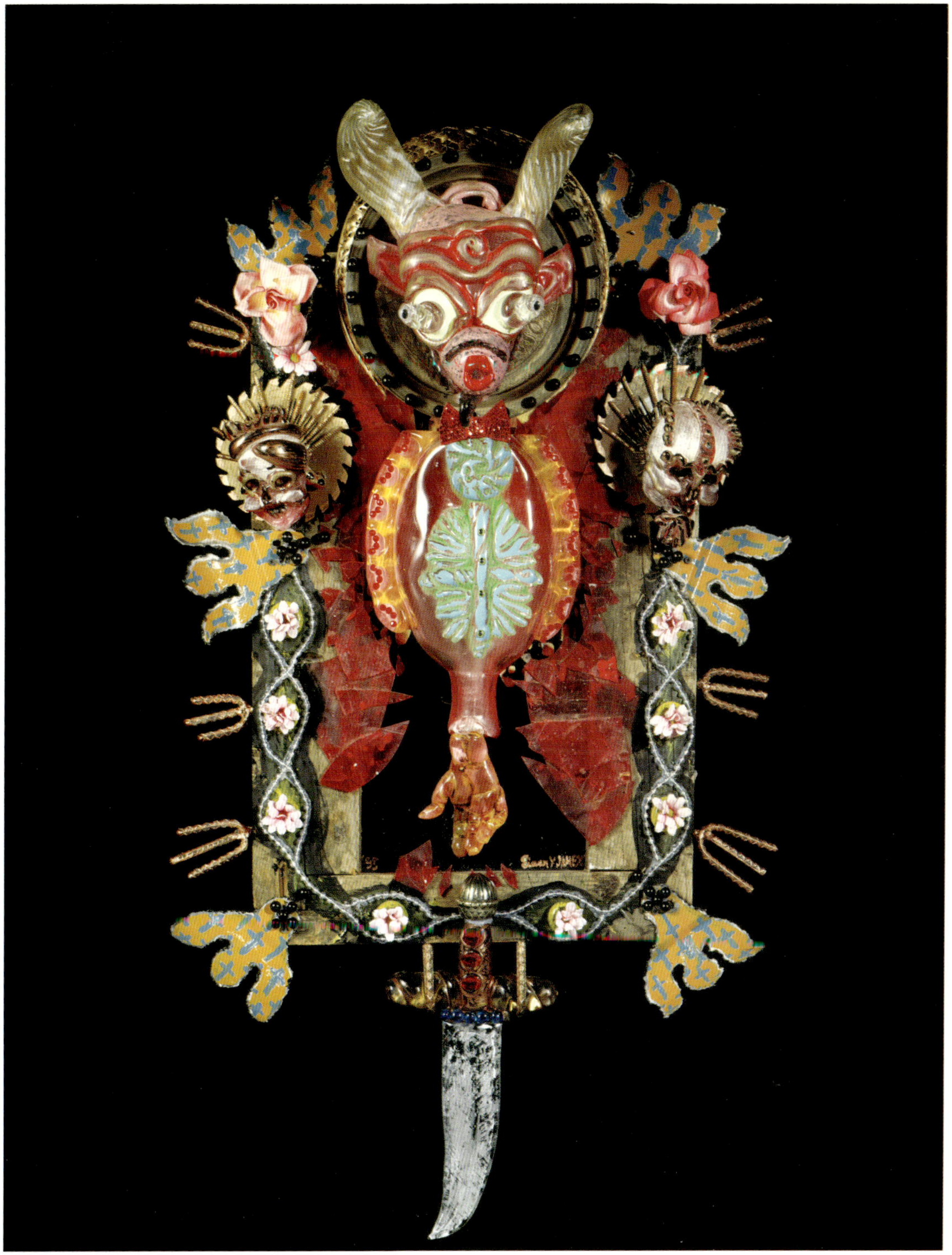

Einar and Jamex collaboration
El Chamuco y sus Jefecitos, 1995
Mixed media with blown glass
54 x 31 x 16
Collection of John Venator, Chicago, Il

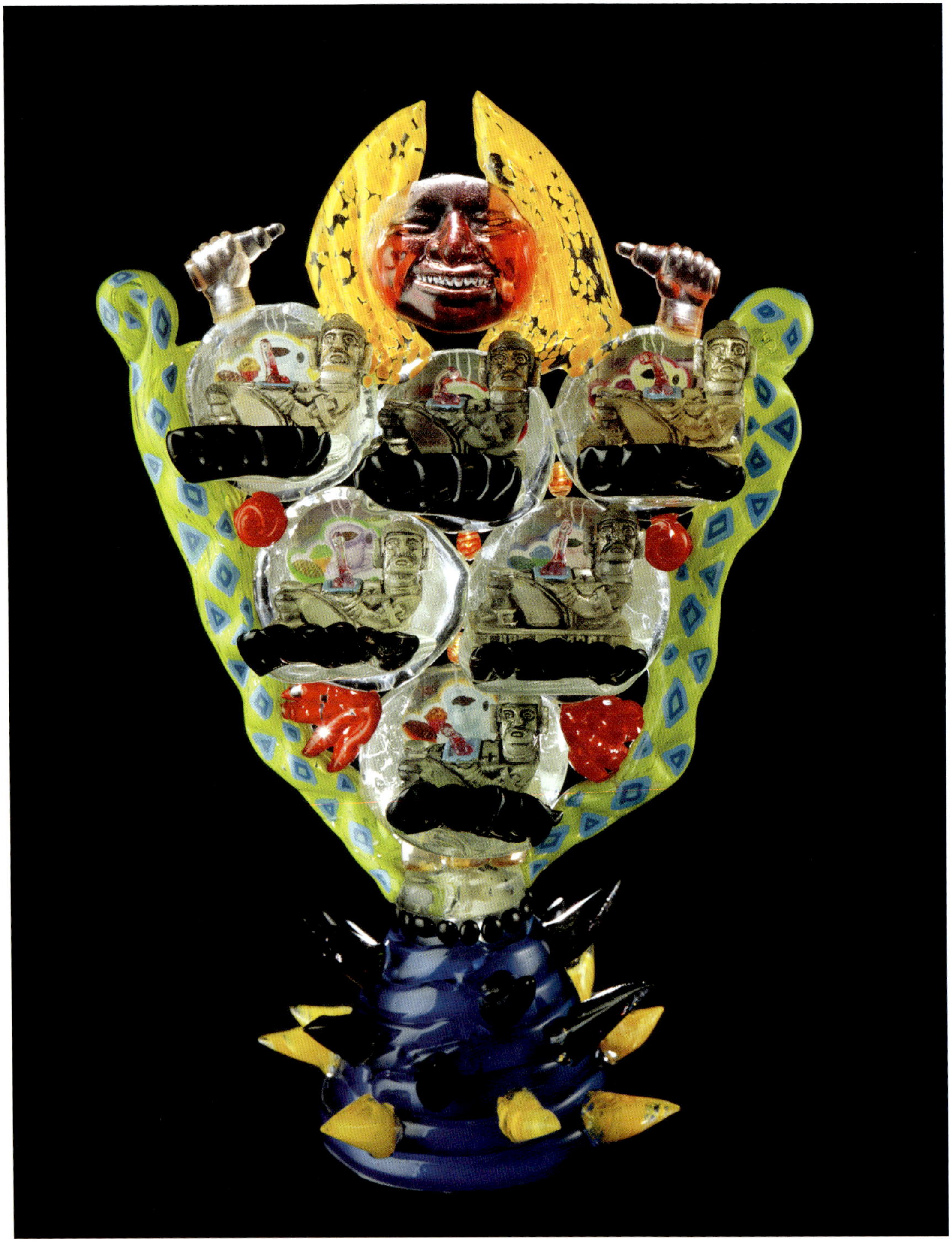

Einar and Jamex collaboration
El Chupon de Dios, 2001
Mixed media with blown glass
24 x 17 x 10

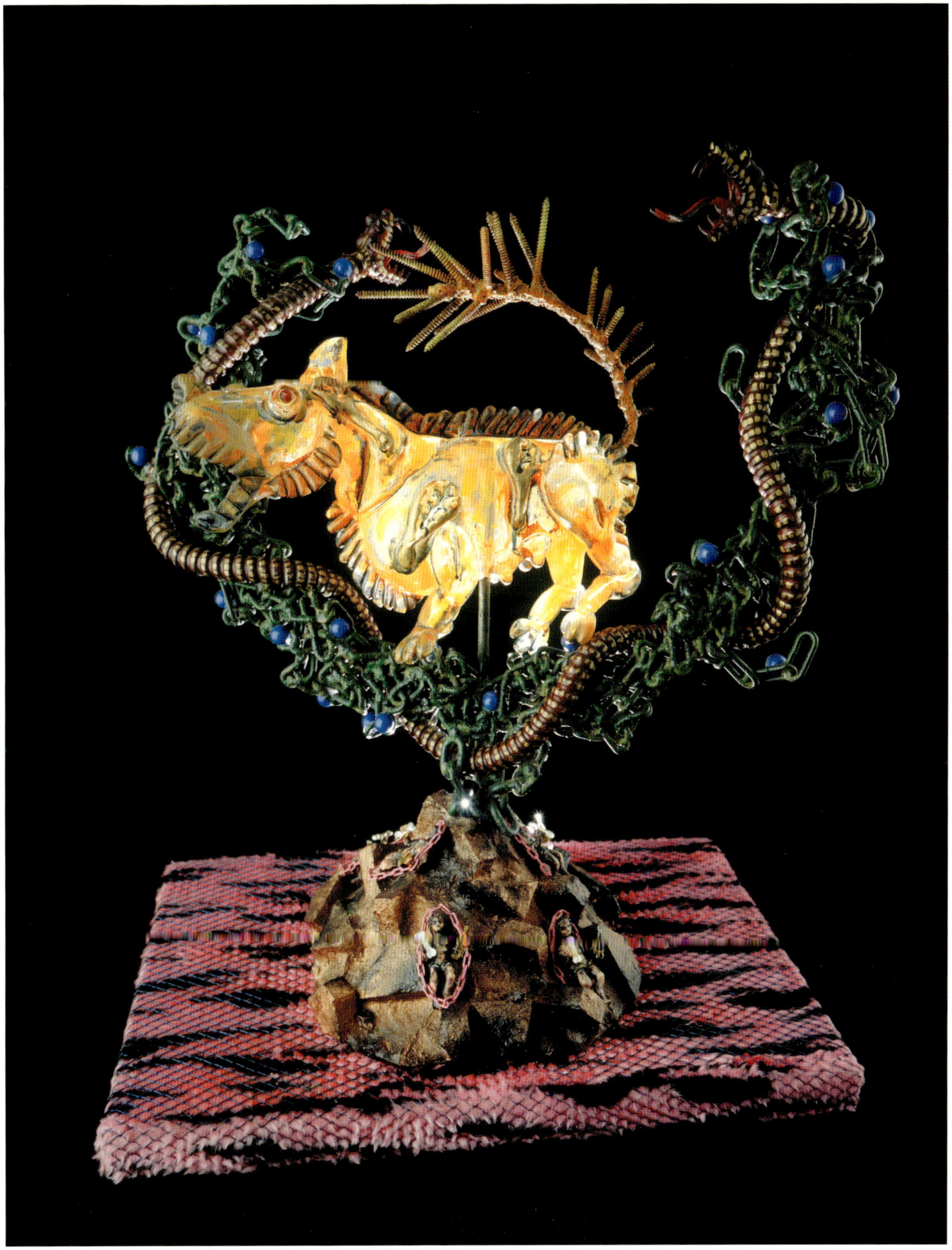

Jamex de la Torre
Perra Patria, 1996
Mixed media with blown glass
28 x 26 x 13

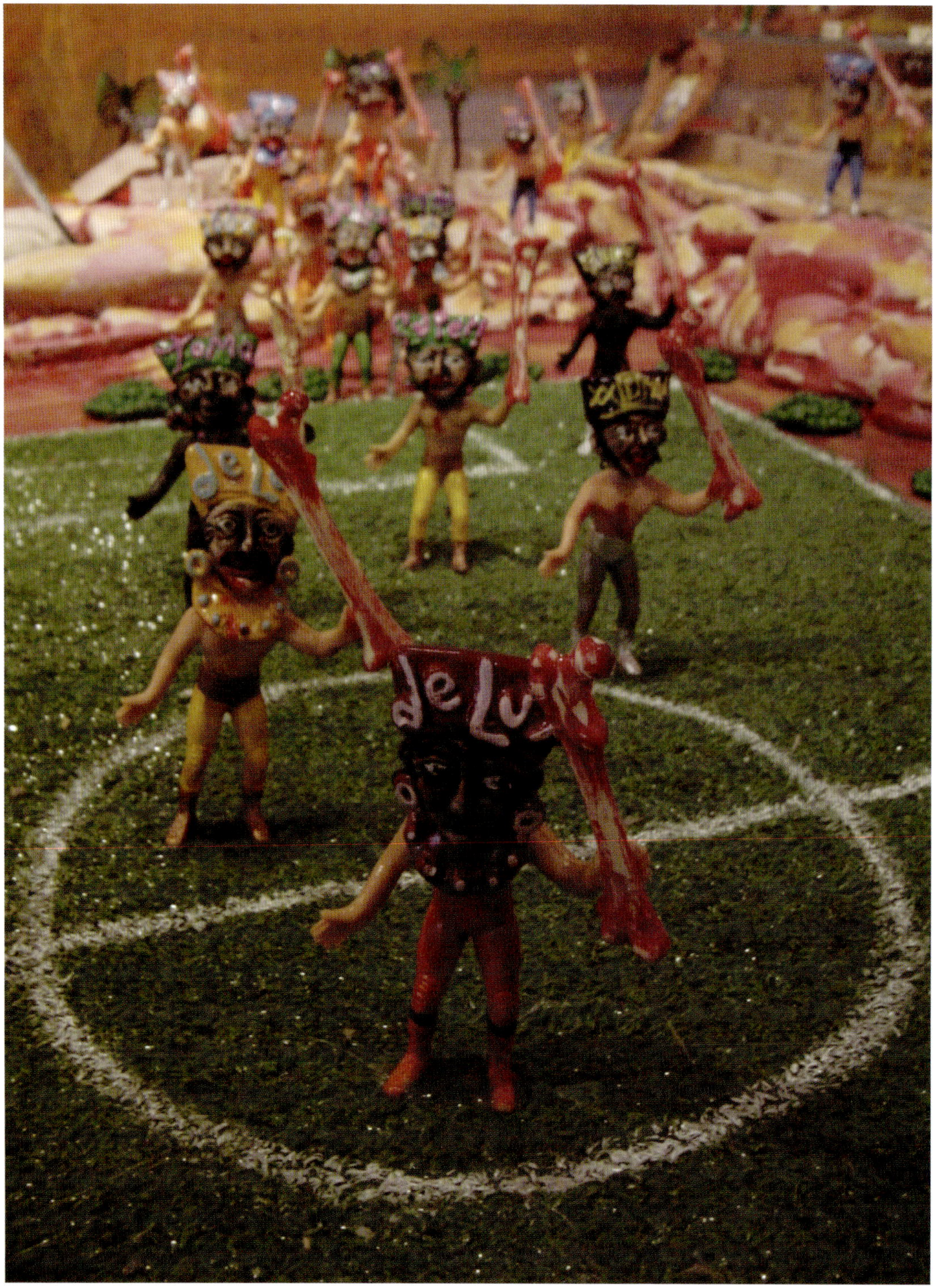

Conquistando installation detail
Anacronistas, 2001
Grand Arts, Kansas City, MO
Curated by Sean Kelley

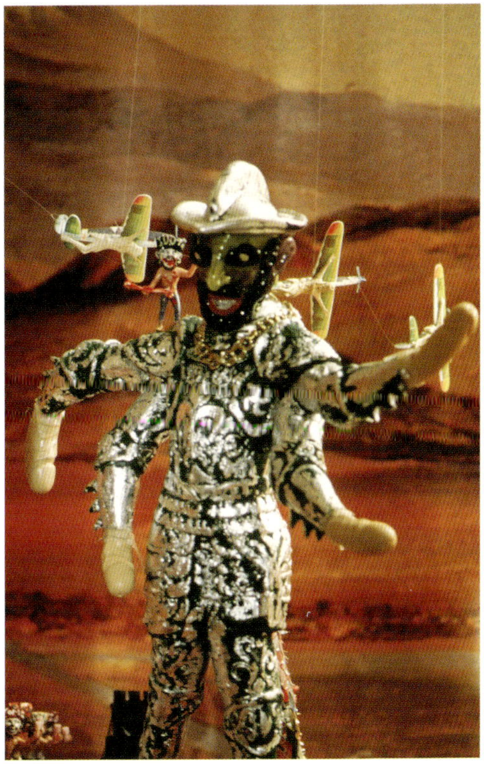

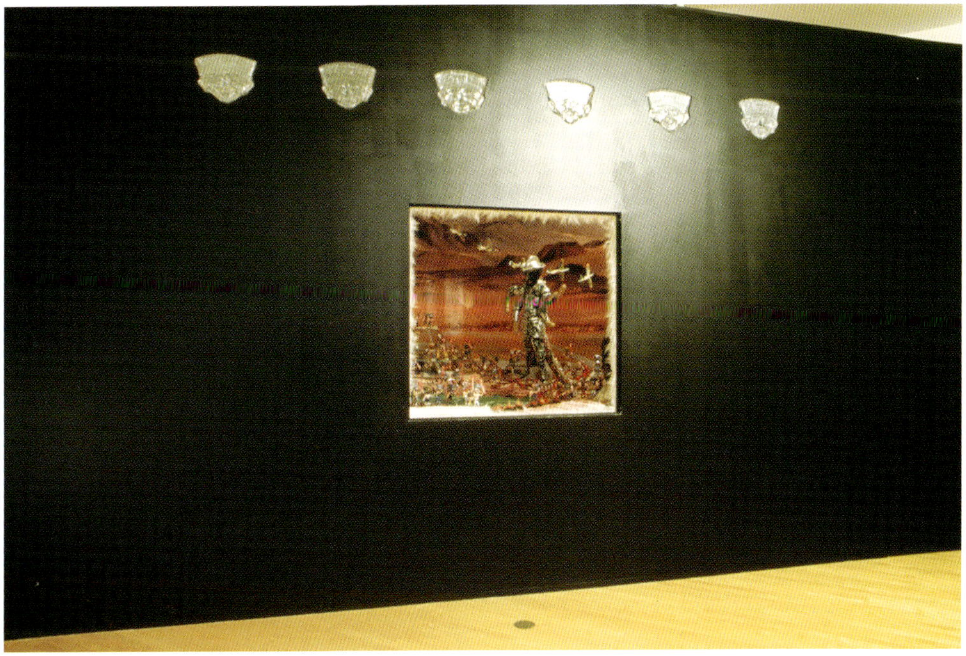

Conquistando installation detail

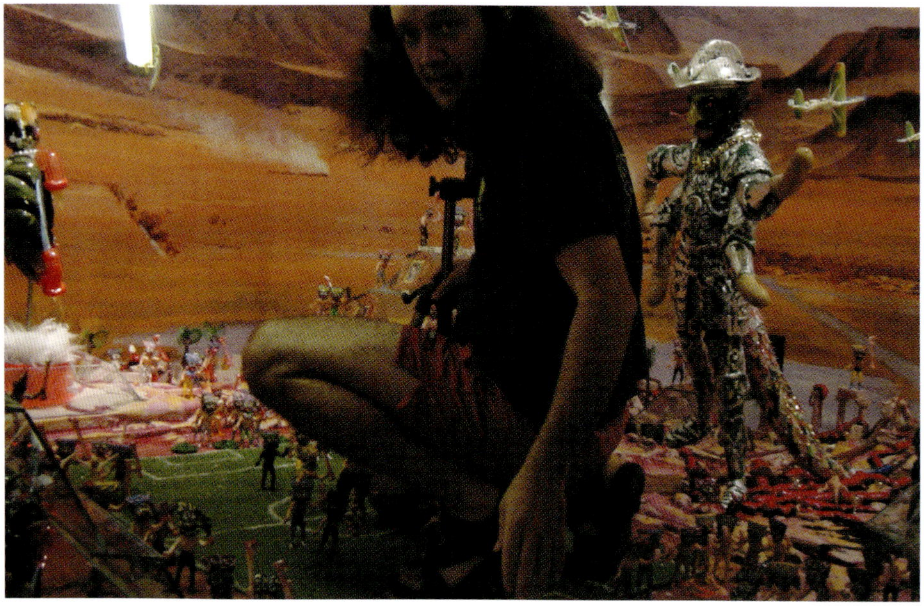

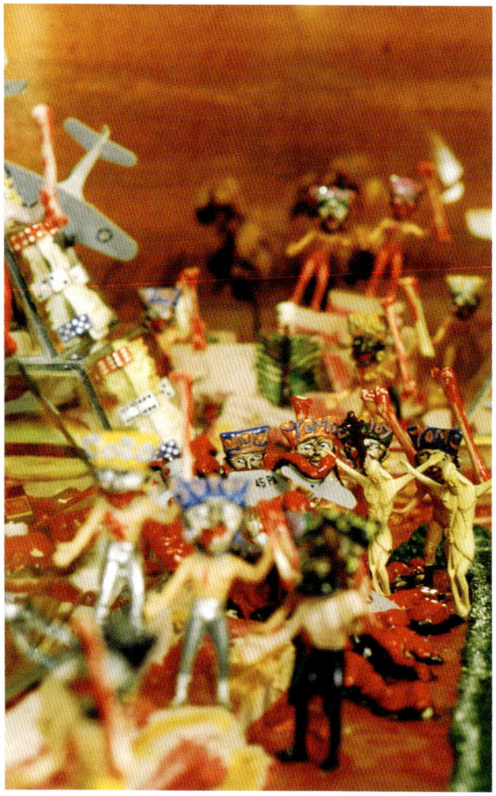

Conquistando installation details
Anacronistas, 2001
Grand Arts Kansas City, MO.
Curated by Sean Kelley

Right:
Conquistando installation details

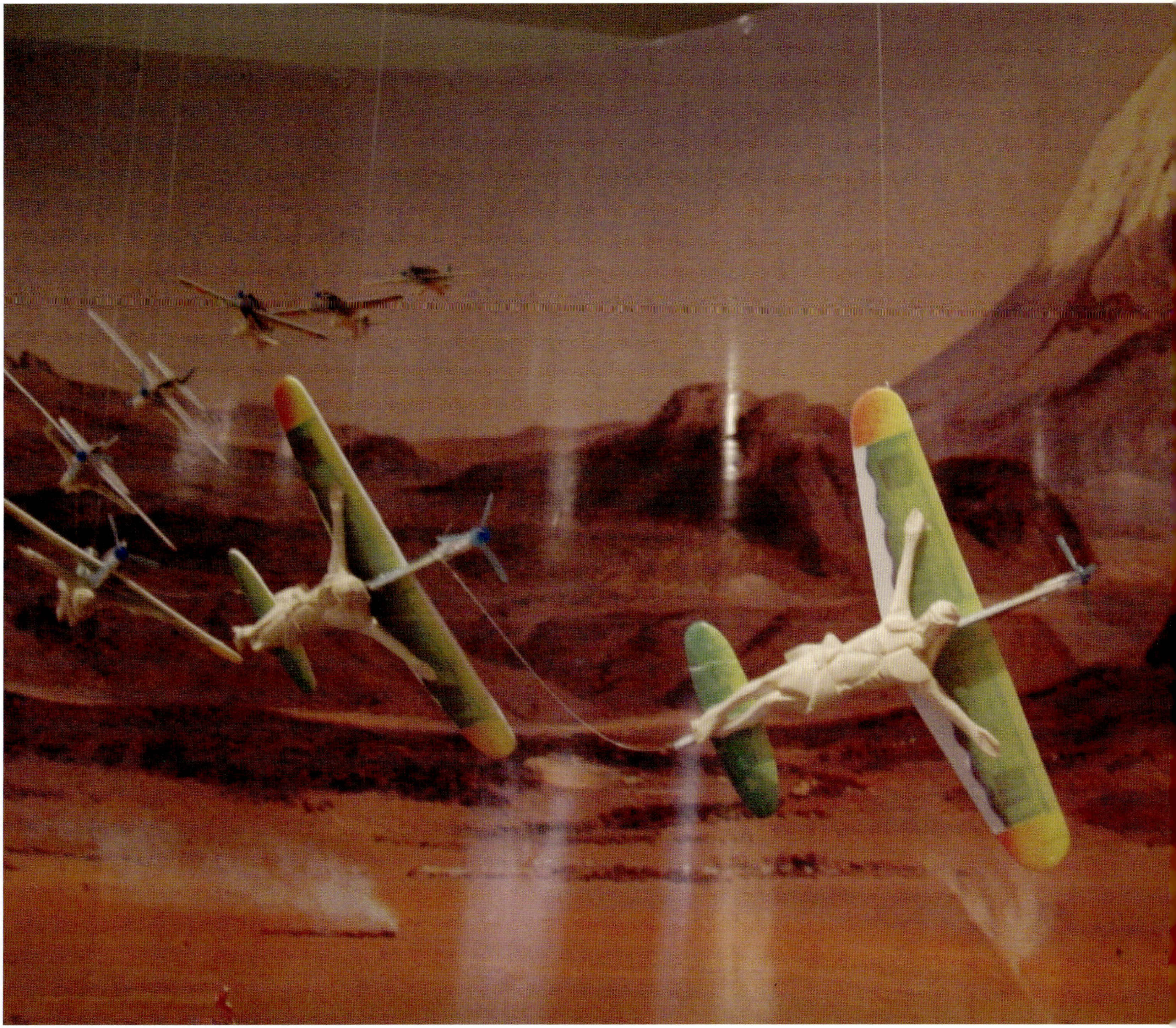

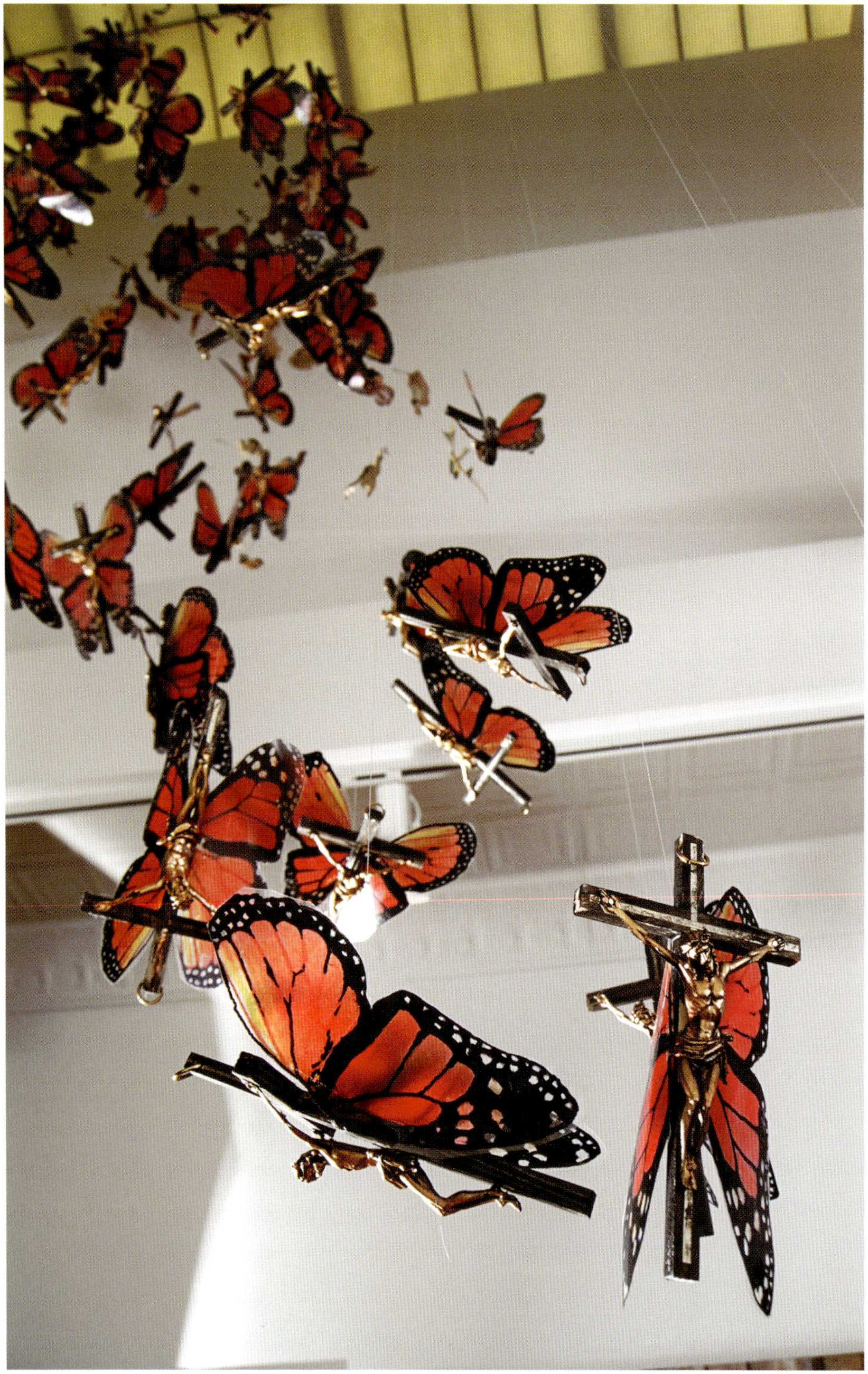

Both images:
Rapture, installation detail
Neorelics: The Spanglish Period-Exhibition
The Salina Art Center, Salina, KS
Curated by Stacy Switzer

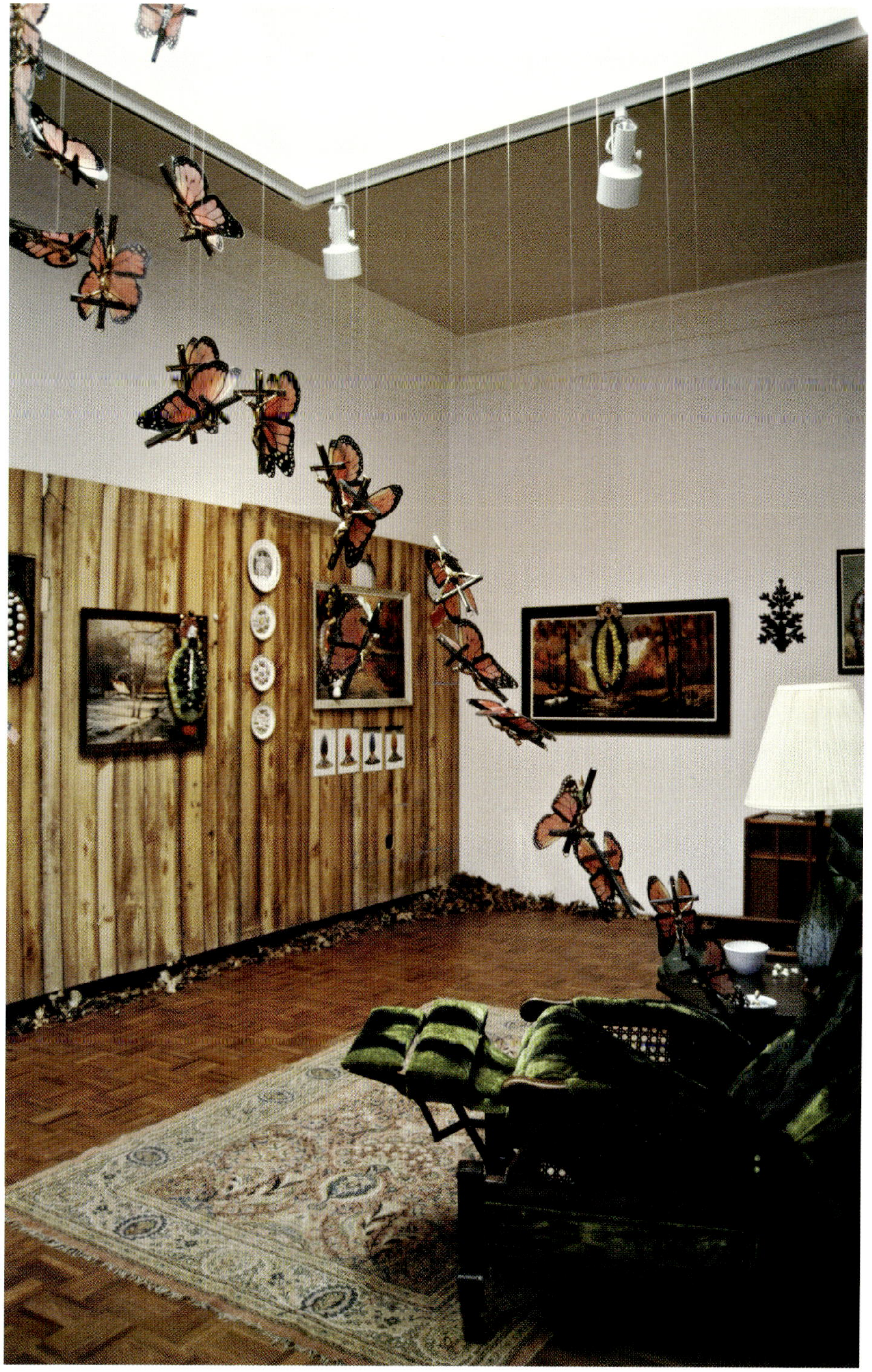

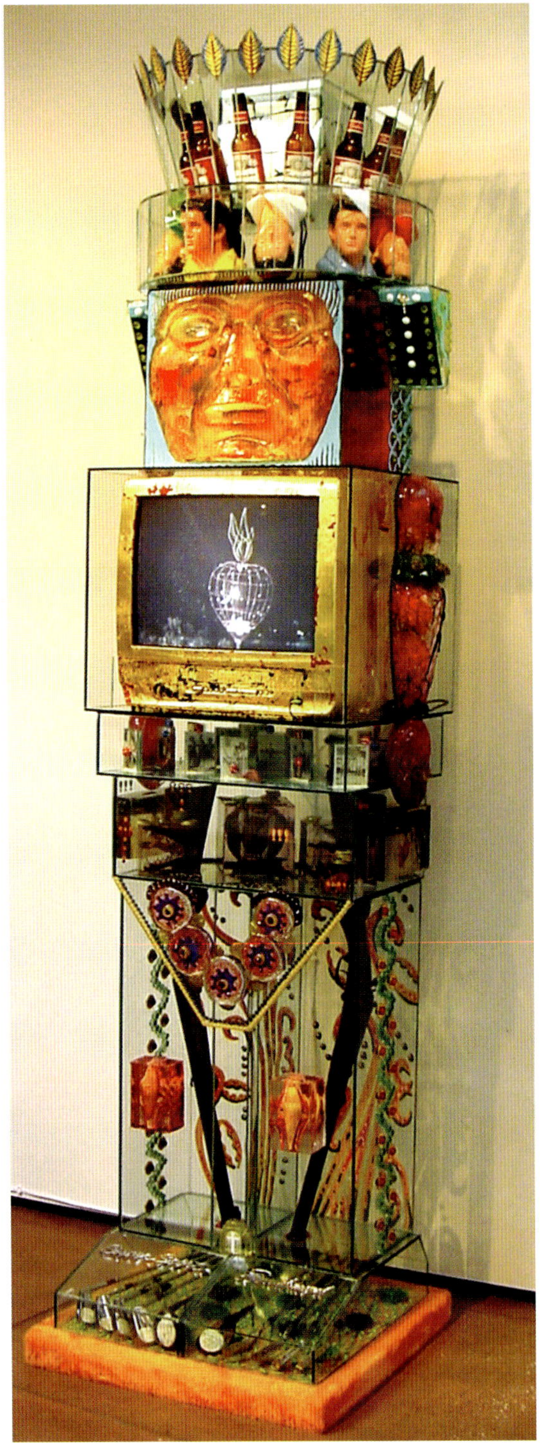

Einar and Jamex collaboration
Tula Norte, 2001
Mixed media with blown glass
113 x 30 x 26

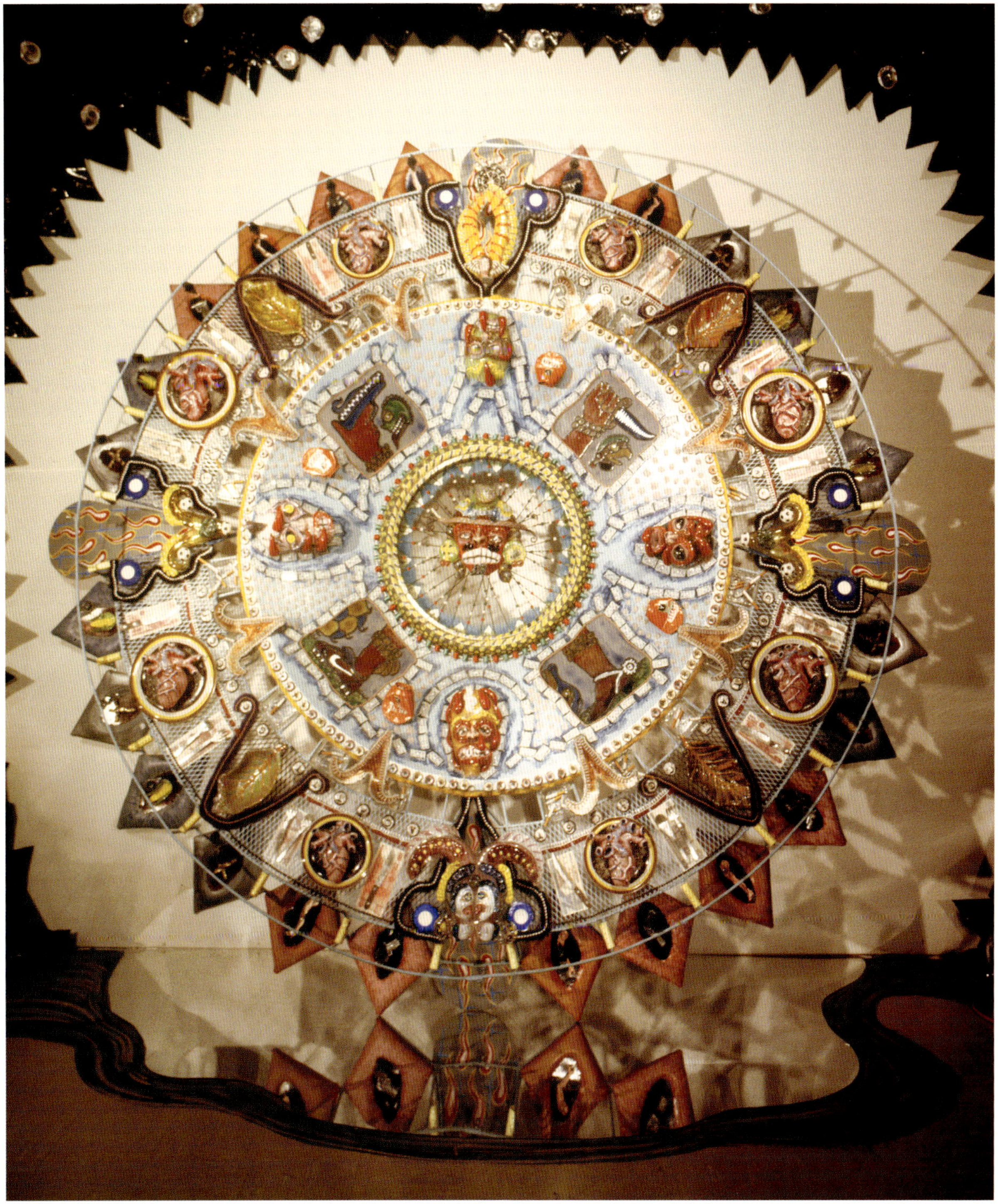

Einar and Jamex collaboration
Installed in El Niño's Wake
Oxymodern, 1999
Mixed media with blown glass
104 diameter
Collection of Cheech Marin

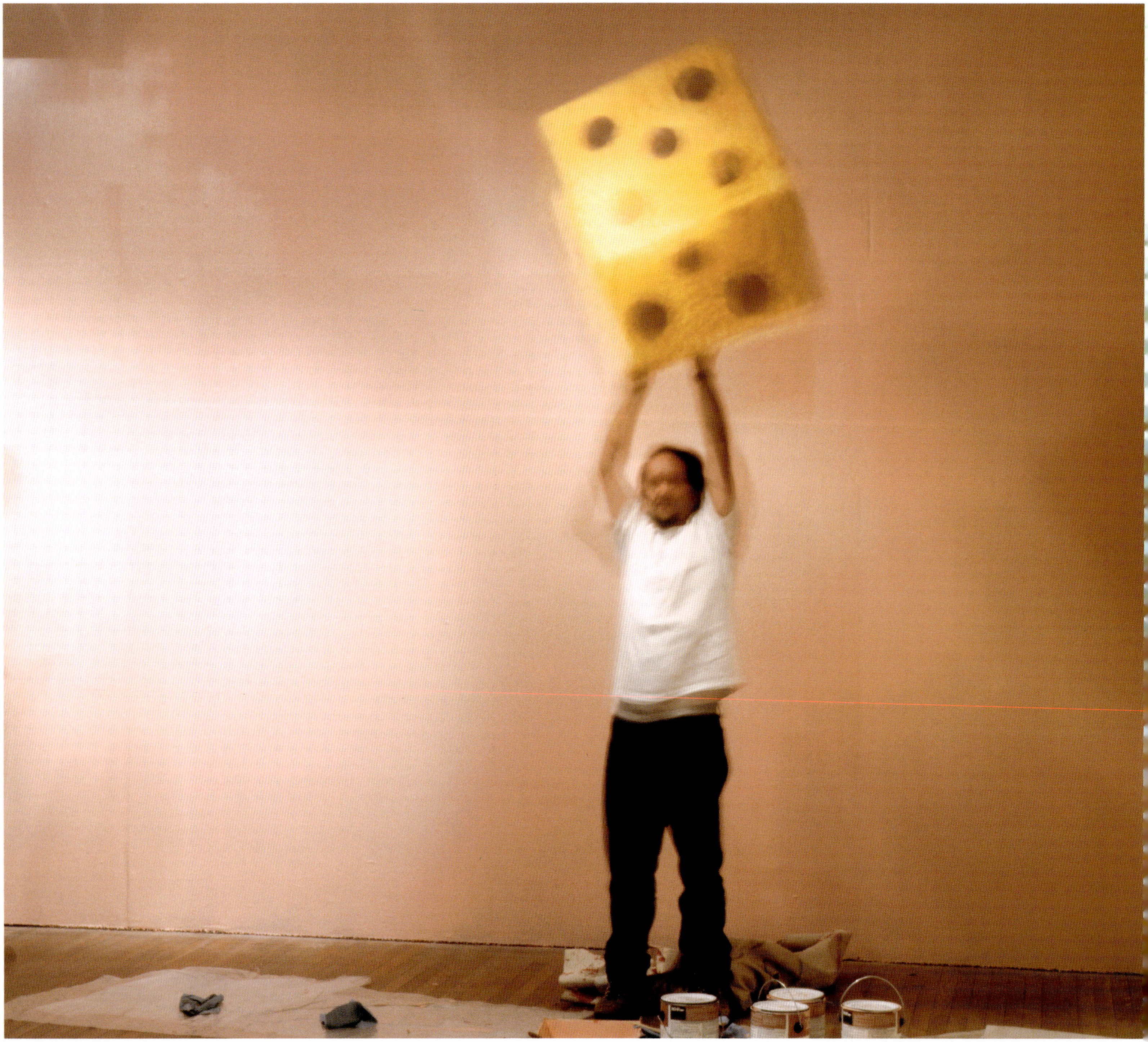

Einar and Jamex de la Torre installing, 2001
Mexic-Arte, Austin, TX

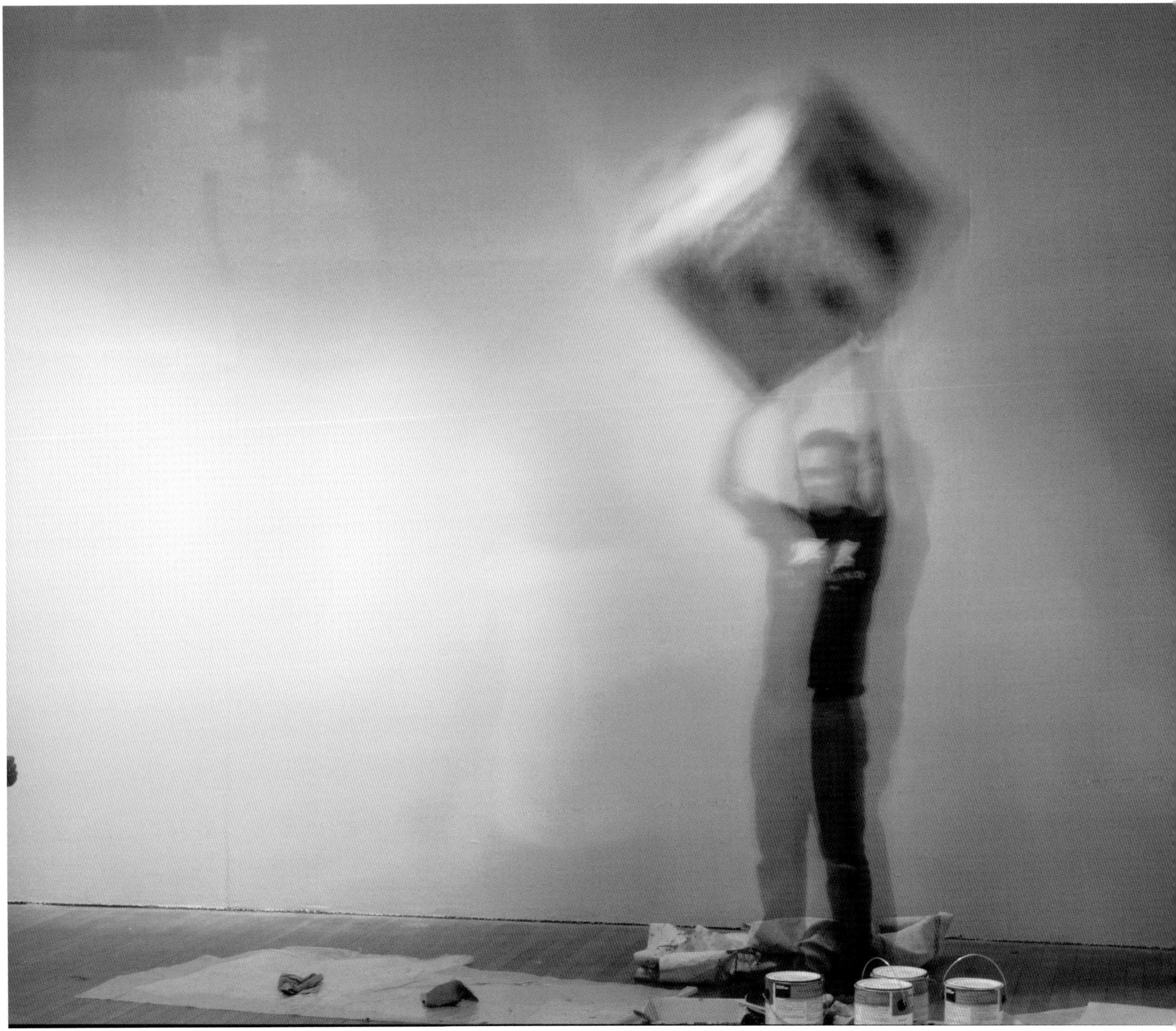

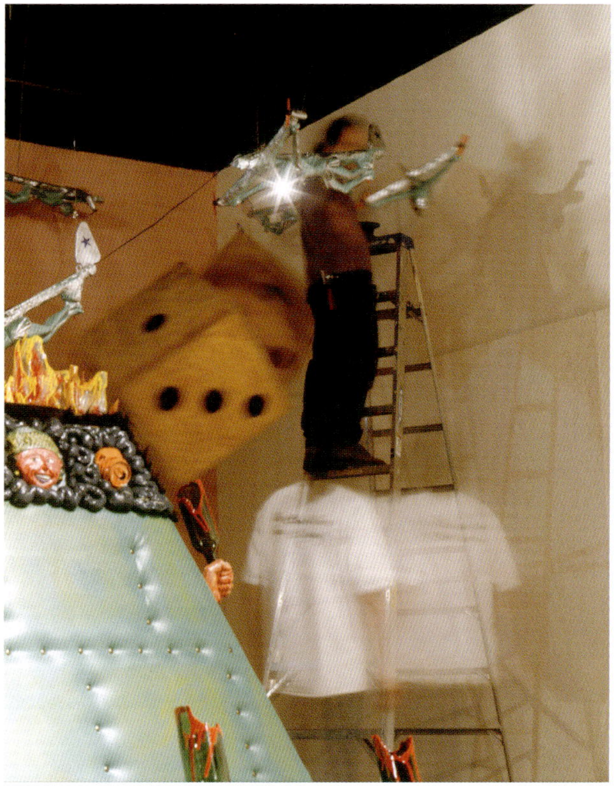

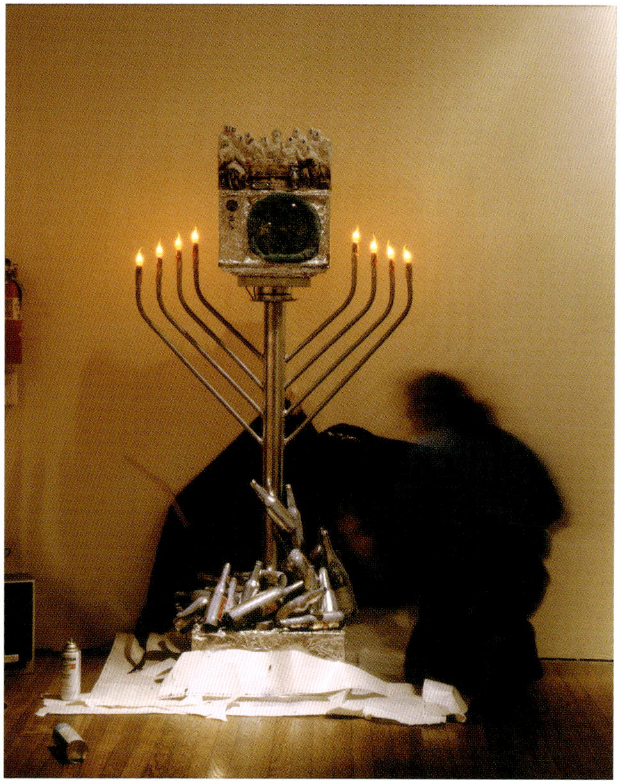

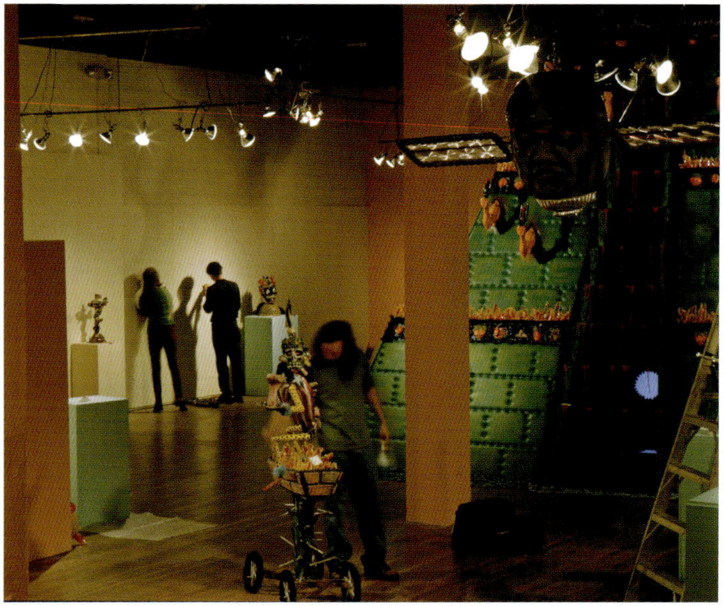

Above:
Einar and Jamex collaboration
Cambio de Canal, 1999
Mixed media
67 x 48 x 13
Installing Mexic-Arte, Austin, TX, 2001

Installing Mexic-Arte, Austin, TX, 2001

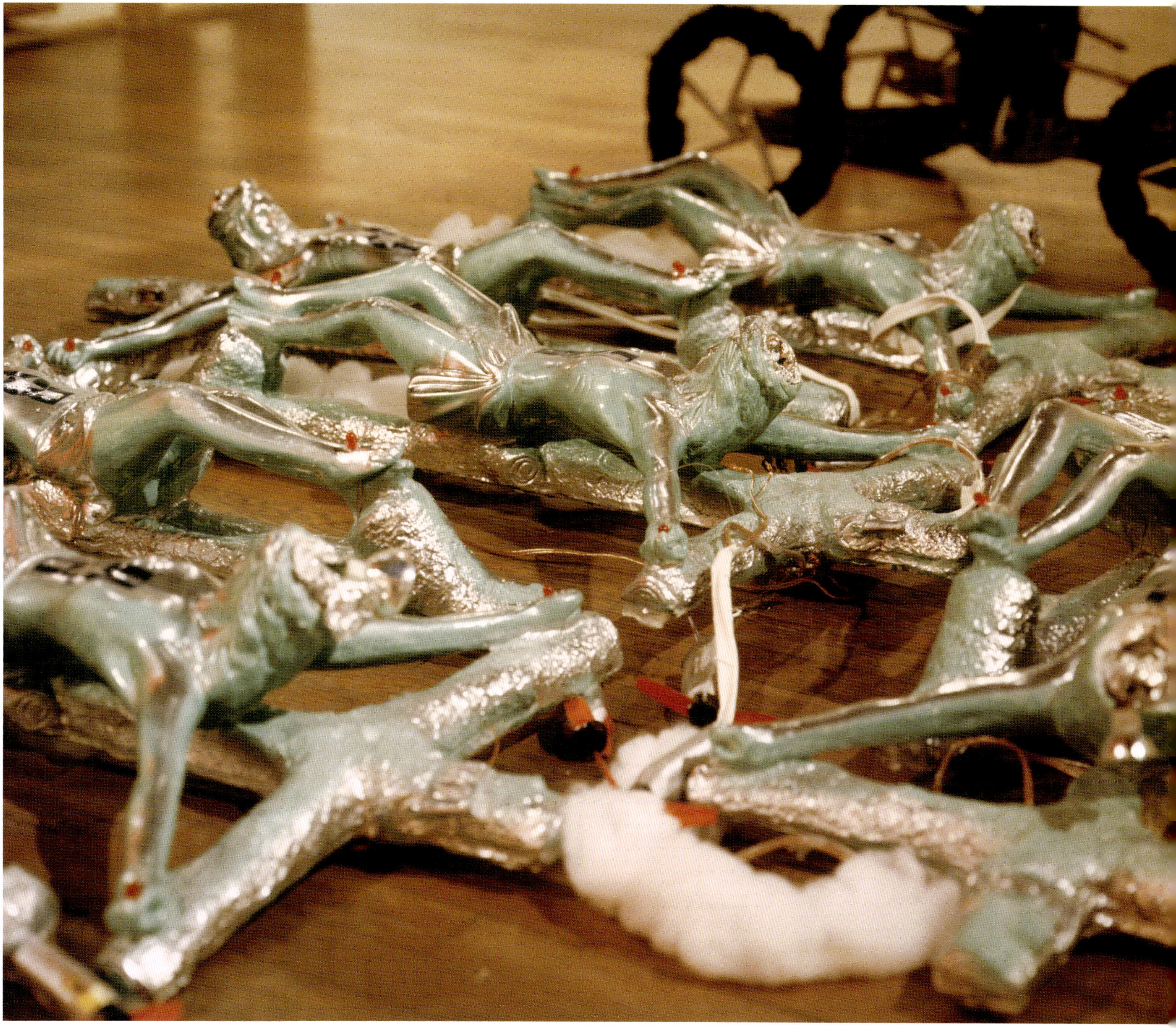

El Nino installation detail

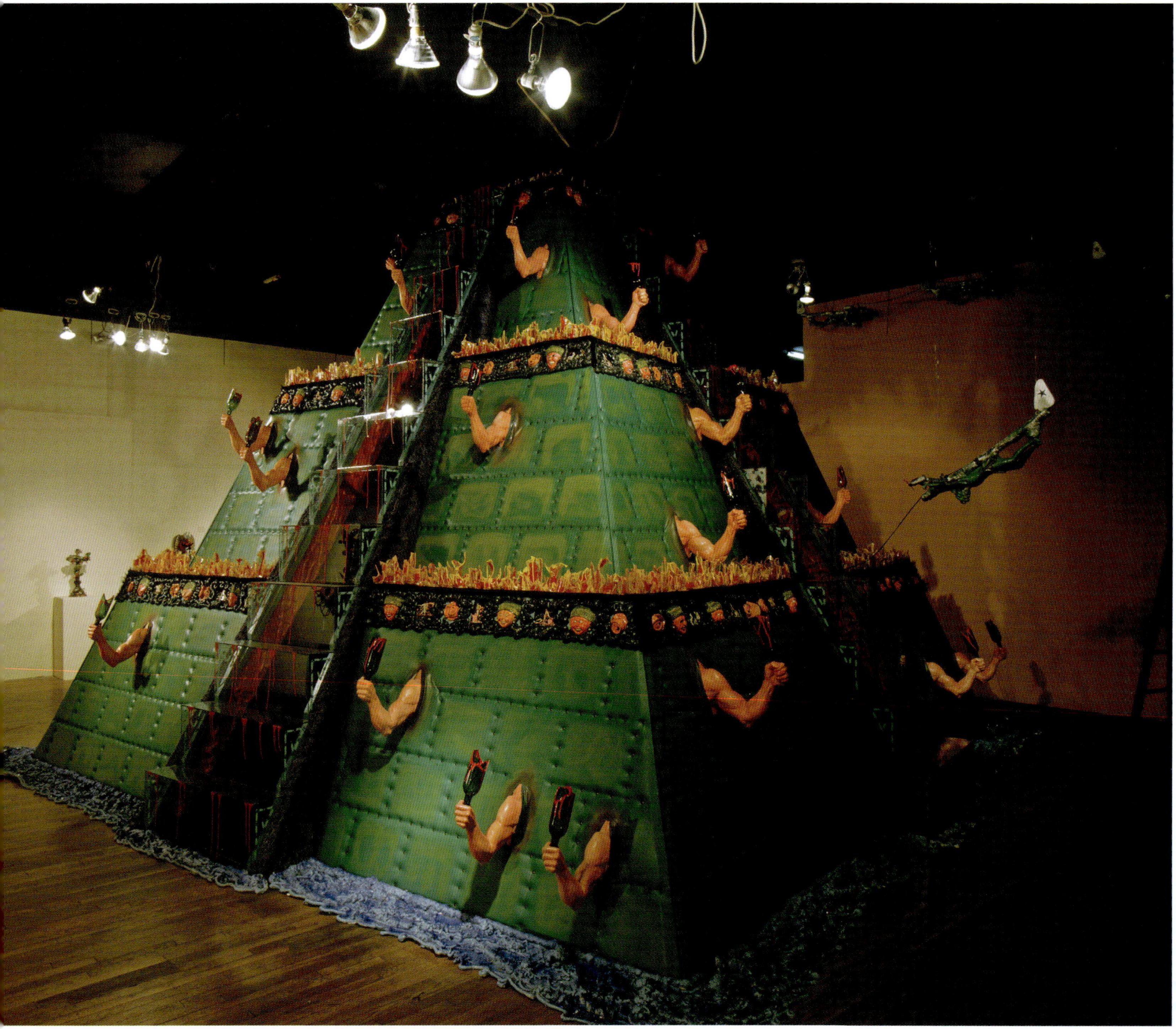

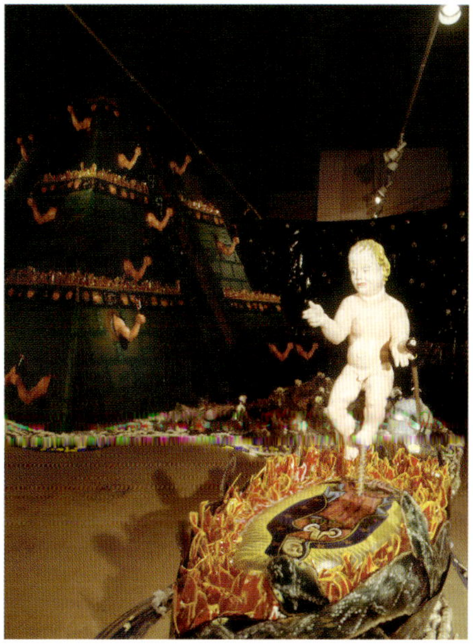

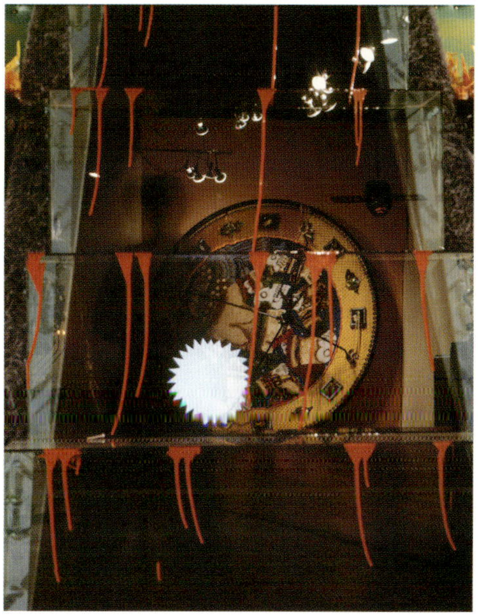

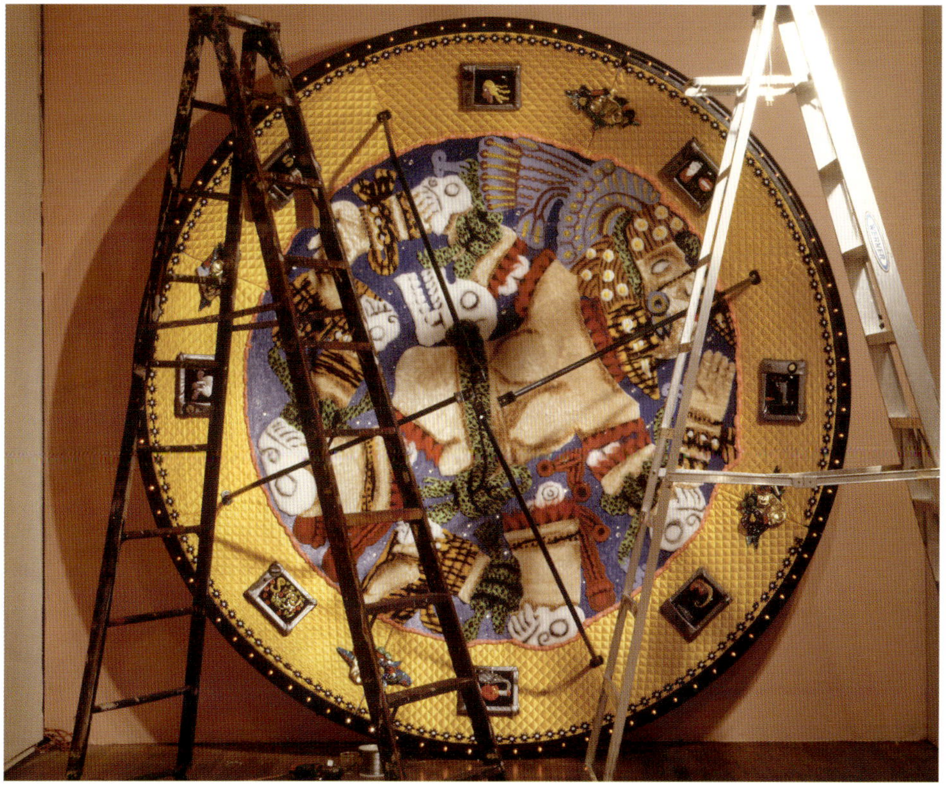

Left:
Einar and Jamex collaboration
El Niño's Wake, 1999
MACLA, San José, CA

Installation details, 2001
Mexic-Arte, Austin, TX

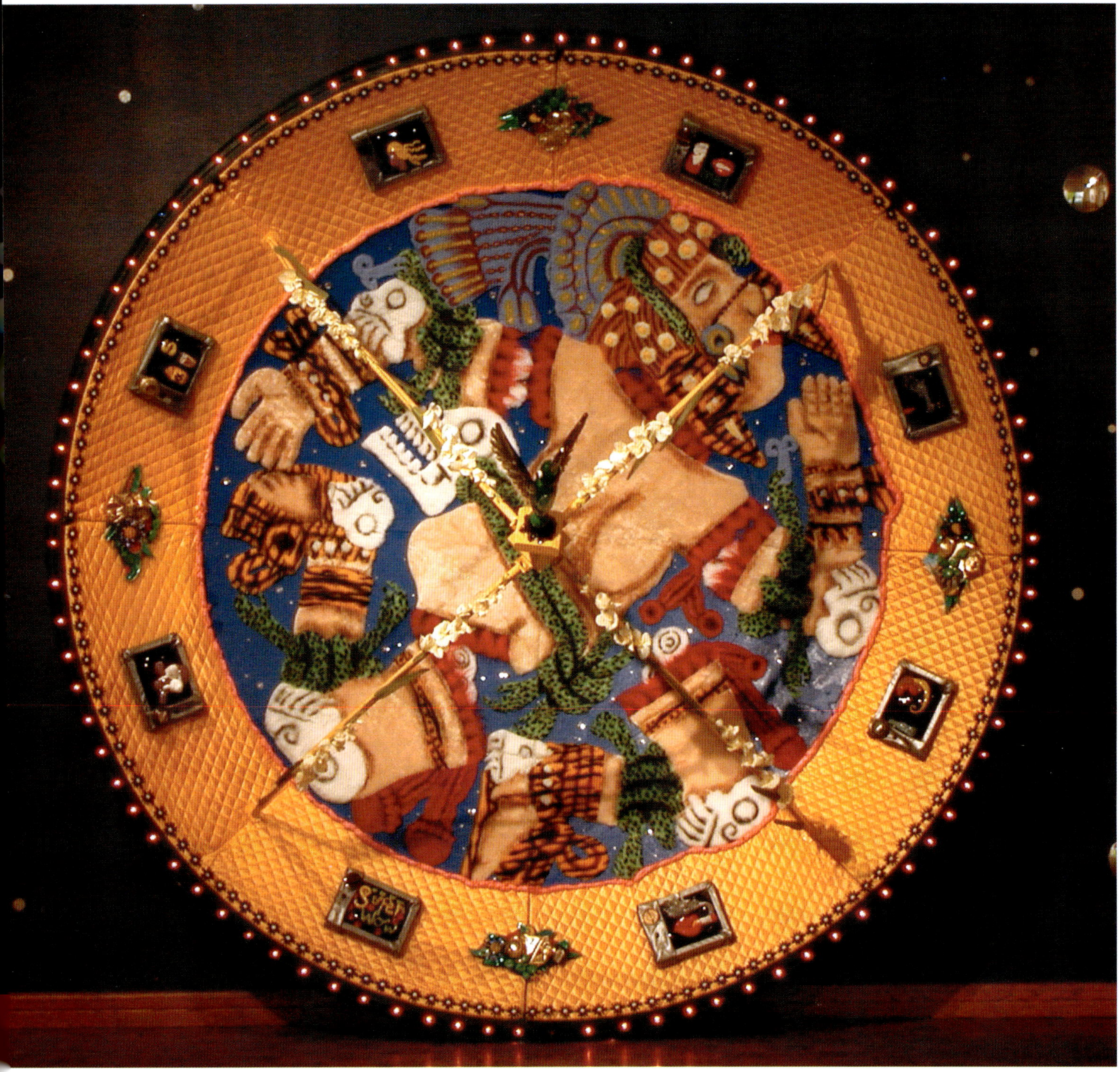

"The immediate-and continuing-impression of the art of the de la Torre brothers, singly and collaboratively, is that of excess, and of risk, of pushing-the-envelope in daredevil flirtation with vulgarity and bombast."

Max Schultz from "Crossing Boundaries" exhibition catalog at USC Fisher Gallery Museum, 2000

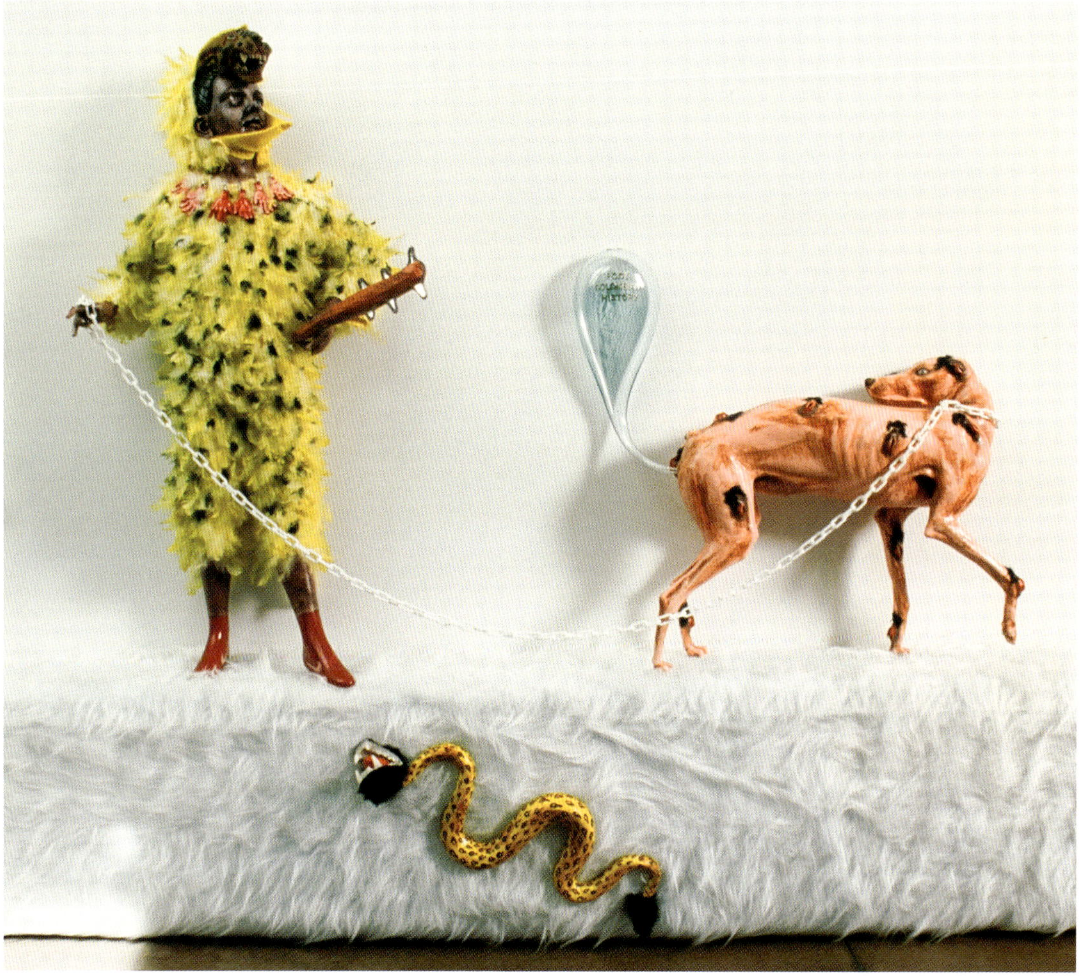

Left:
Einar and Jamex collaboration
Coyo, 2000
Installation
Neorelics: The Spanglish Period
The Salina Art Center, Salina, KS
Curated by Stacy Switzer

Einar and Jamex collaboration
Post Colombian History, 2001
Mixed media with blown glass
70 x 98 x 16

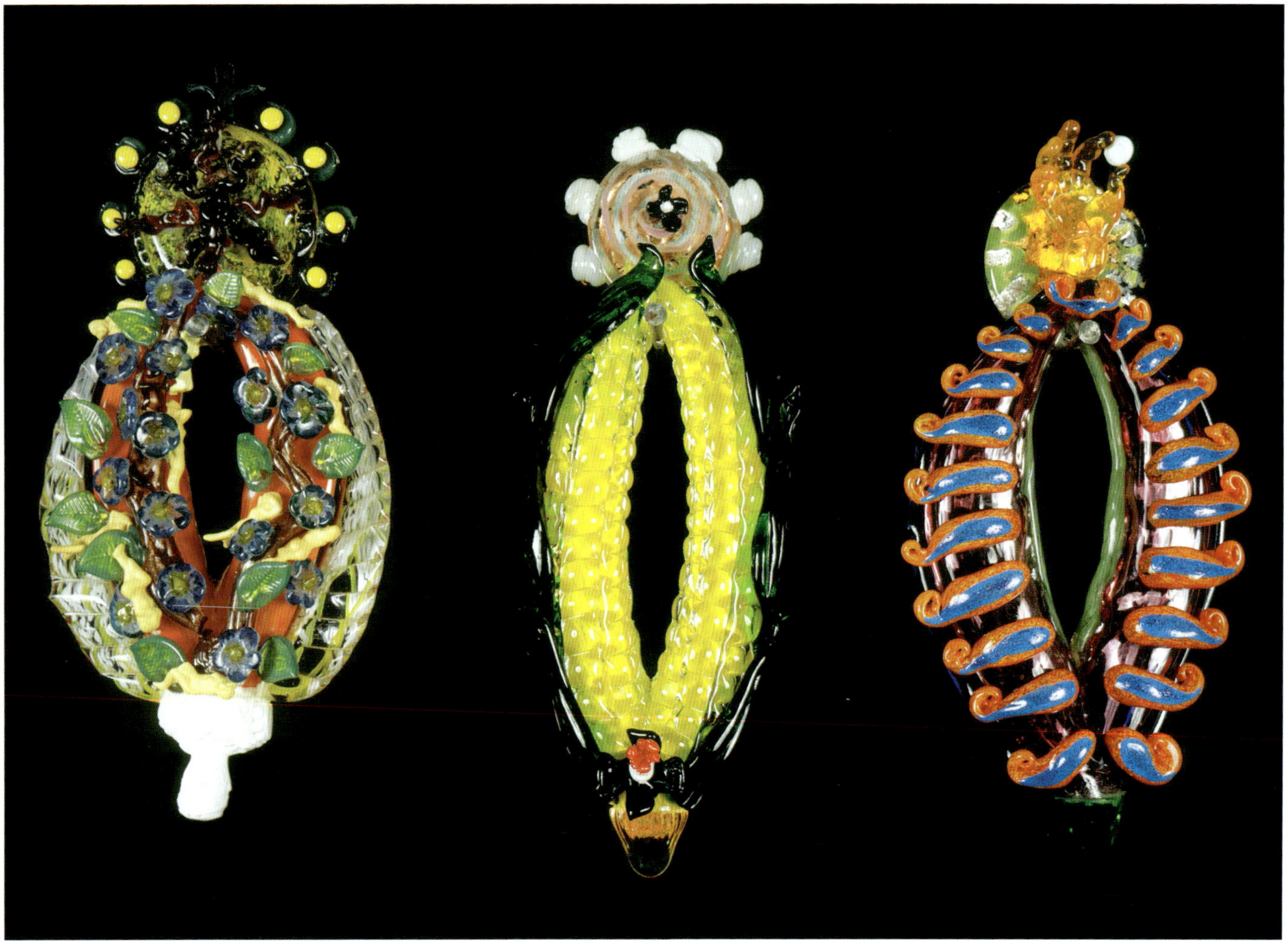

Einar and Jamex collaboration
VirgenVagina Series, 2000-04
Mixed media with blown glass
Varied dimensions

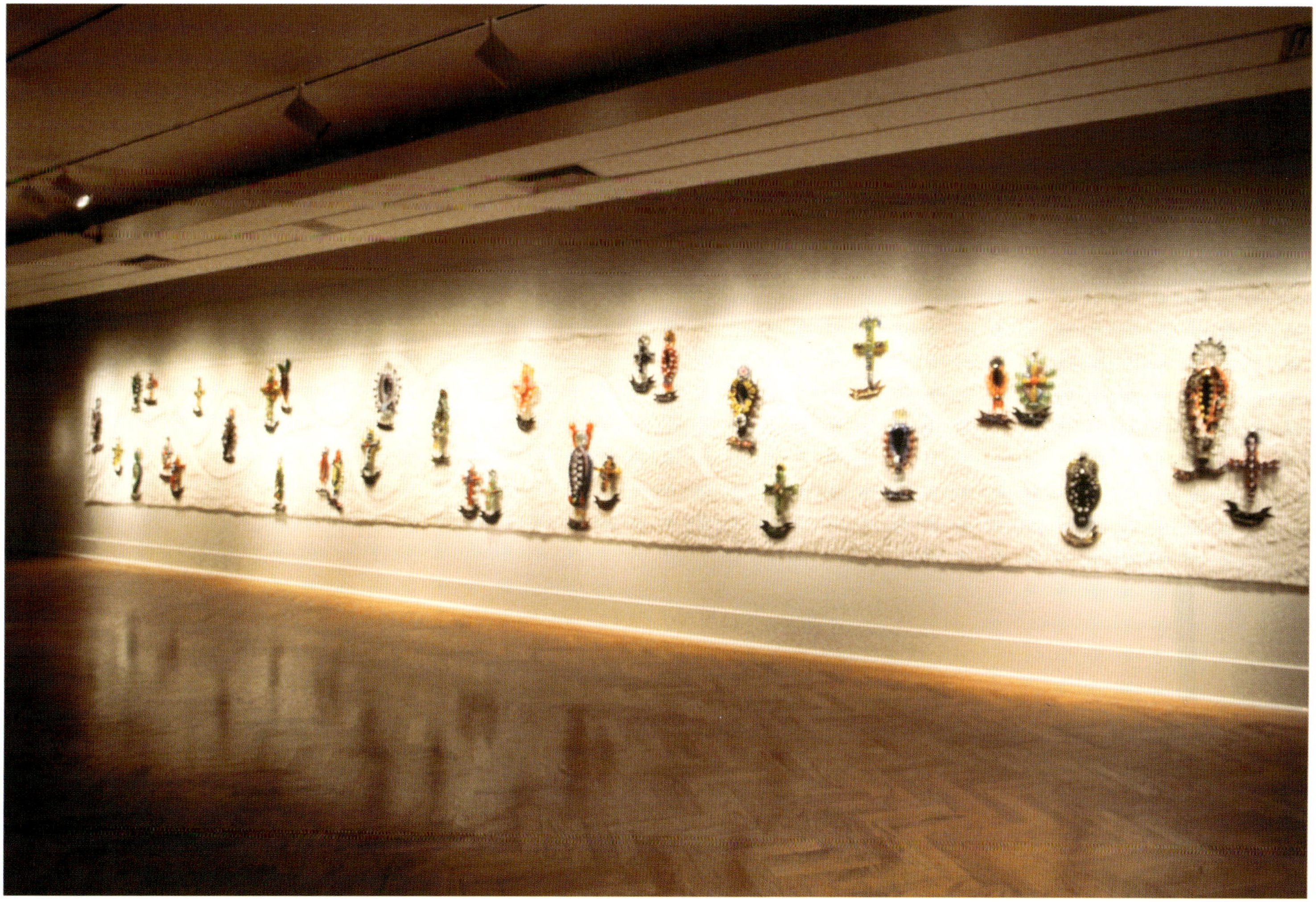

Einar and Jamex collaboration
The Source, 2002
Installation, *Ultrabaroque*
Aspects of Post Latin American Art
Art Gallery of Ontario, Toronto, Canada

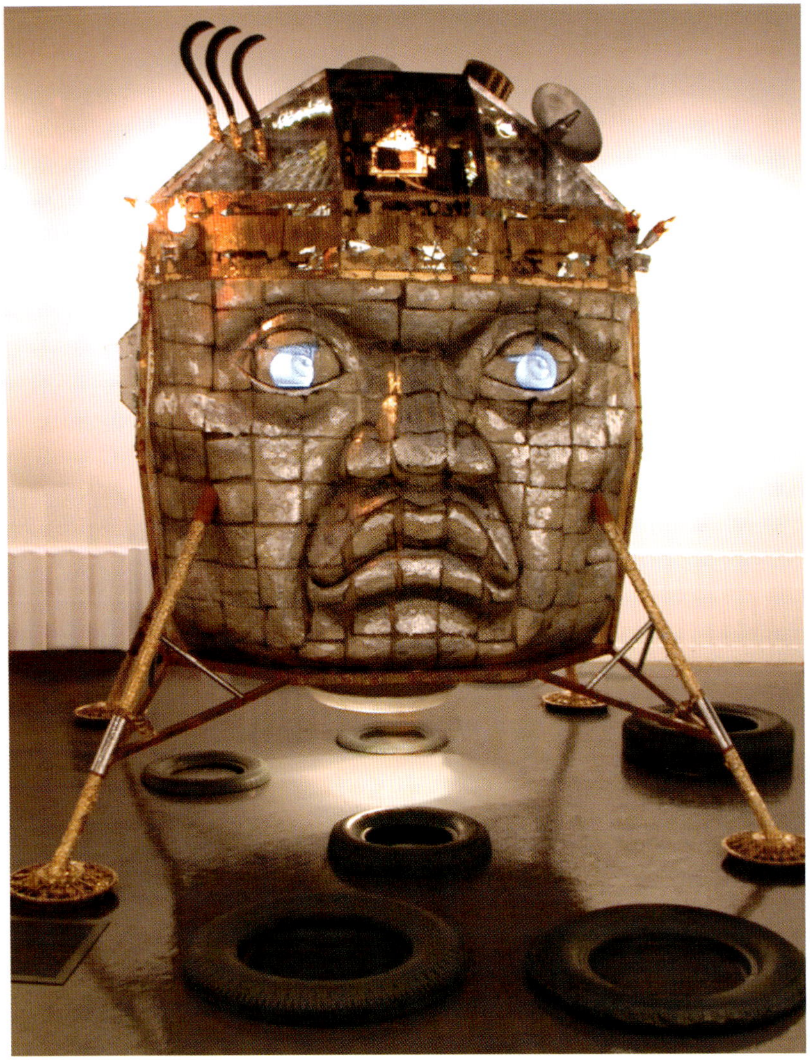

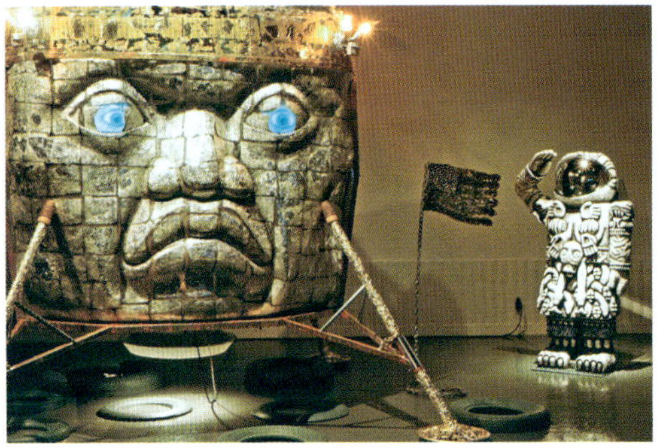

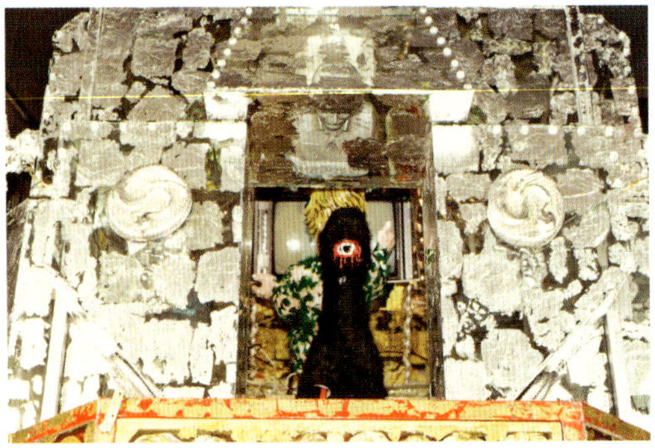

Einar and Jamex collaboration
Colonial Atmosphere, 2002
Installation, *Mixed Feelings*
USC Fisher Gallery, Los Angeles, CA
Curated by Gustavo Leclerc and Michael Dear

Right:
Einar and Jamex collaboration
Maybe, 2002
Mixed media installation including
Quincy Troupe video performance
Museo de las Artes, Guadalajara, Mexico
Curated by Ricardo Duarte

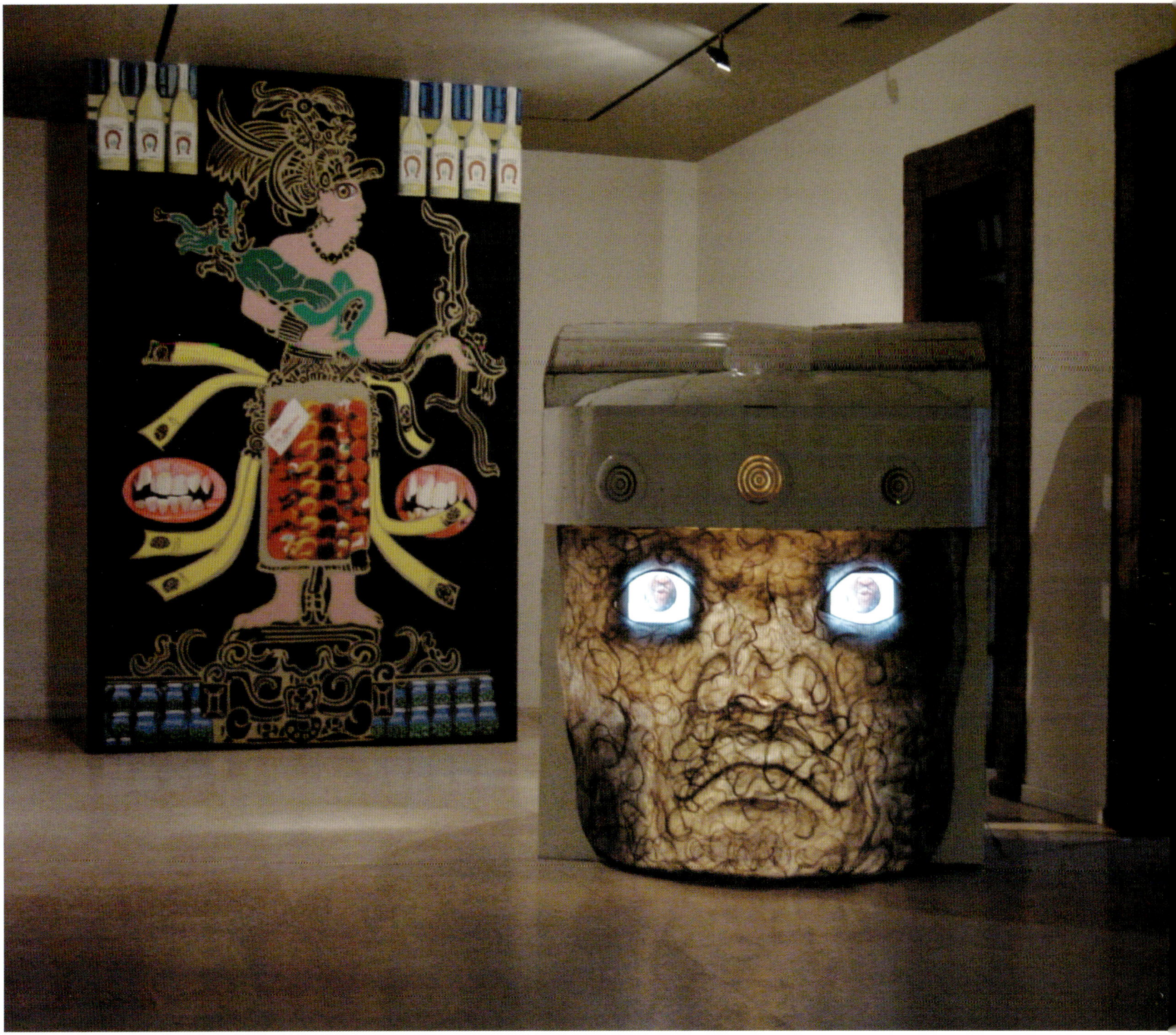

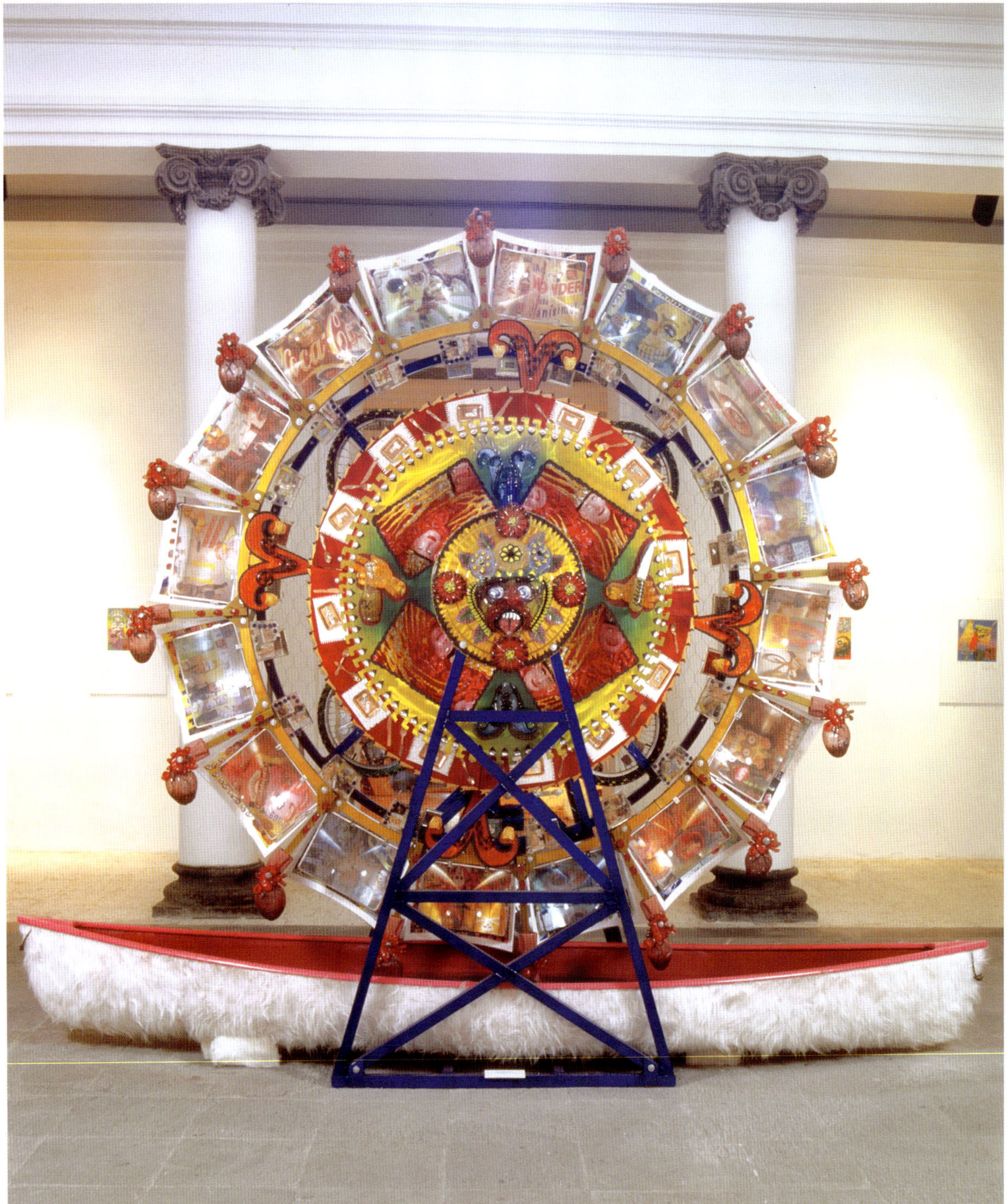

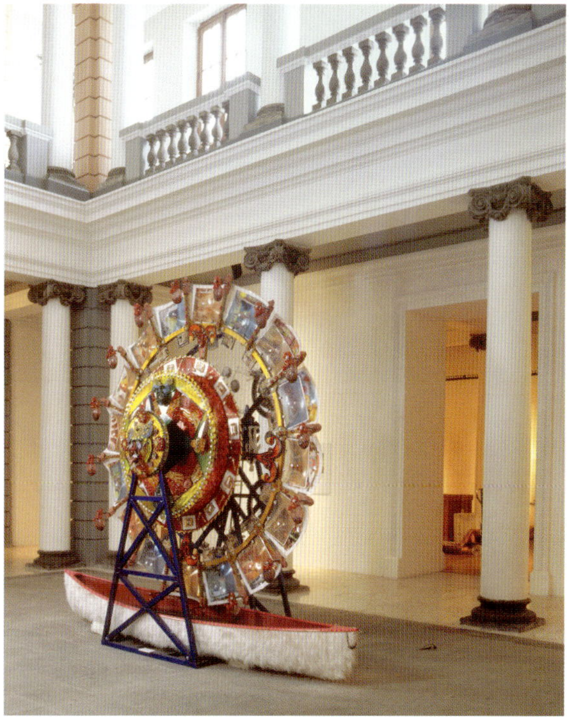

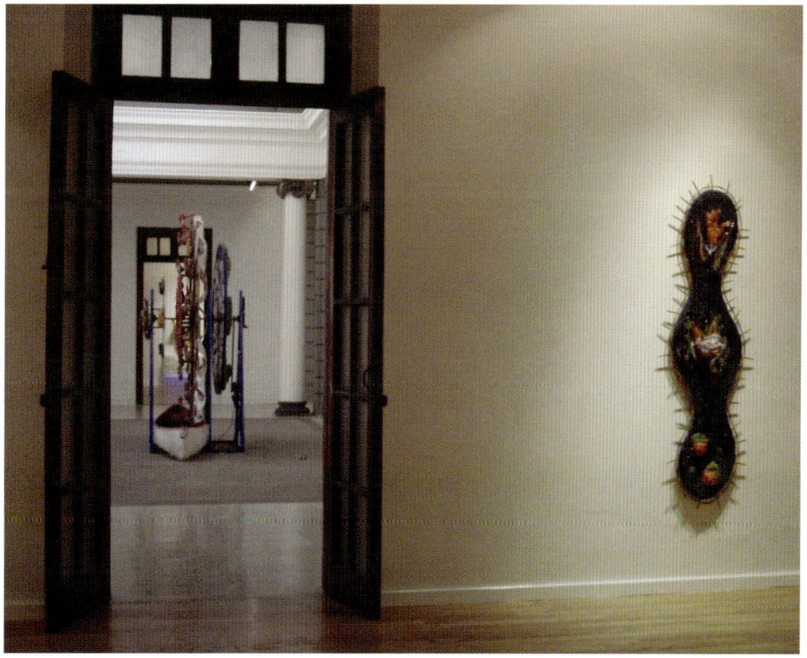

Left:
Einar and Jamex collaboration
La Belle Epoch, 2001
Museo de las Artes Guadalajara
Guadalajara, Mexico

detail and lower detail of *Bacteria*
Museo de las Artes Guadalajara
Guadalajara, Mexico

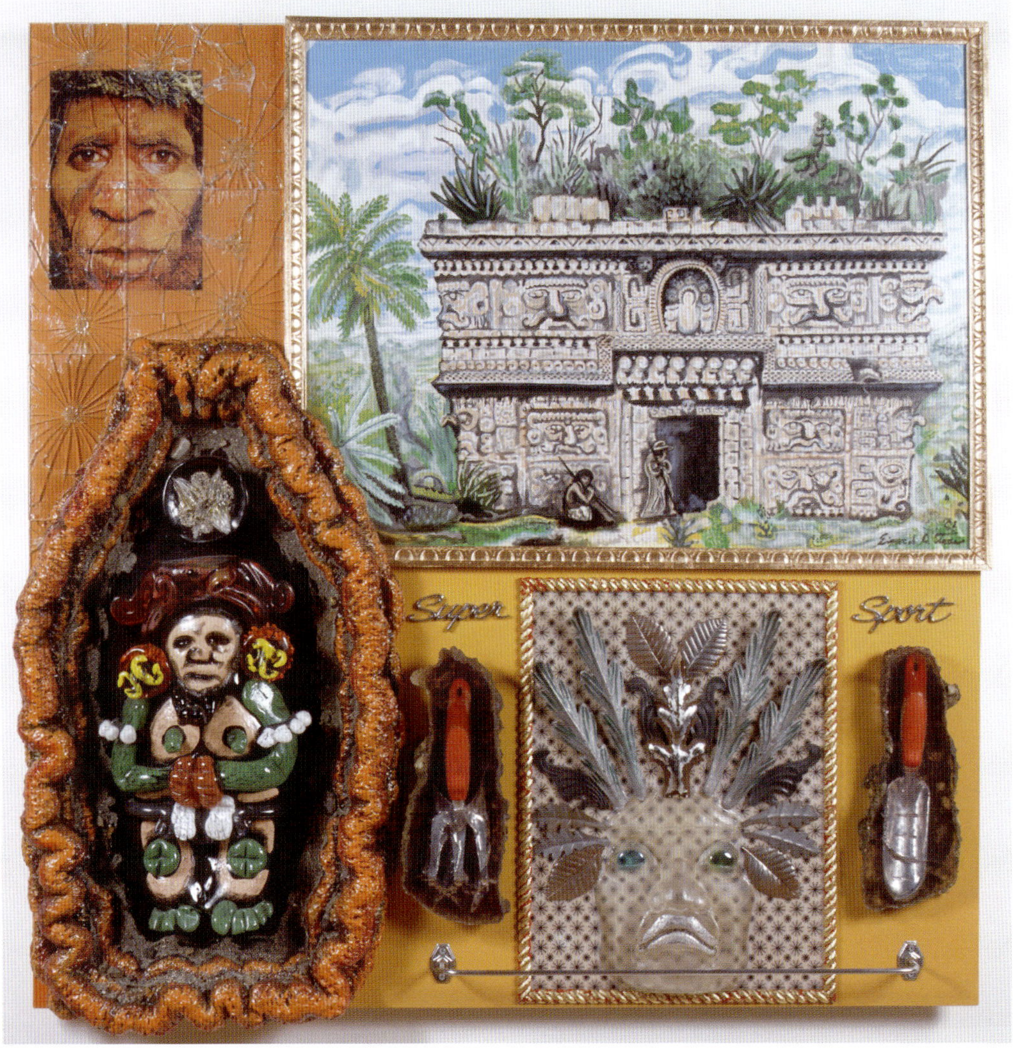

Einar de la Torre
Noble Savage, 2001
Mixed media with blown glass
49 x 49 x 8

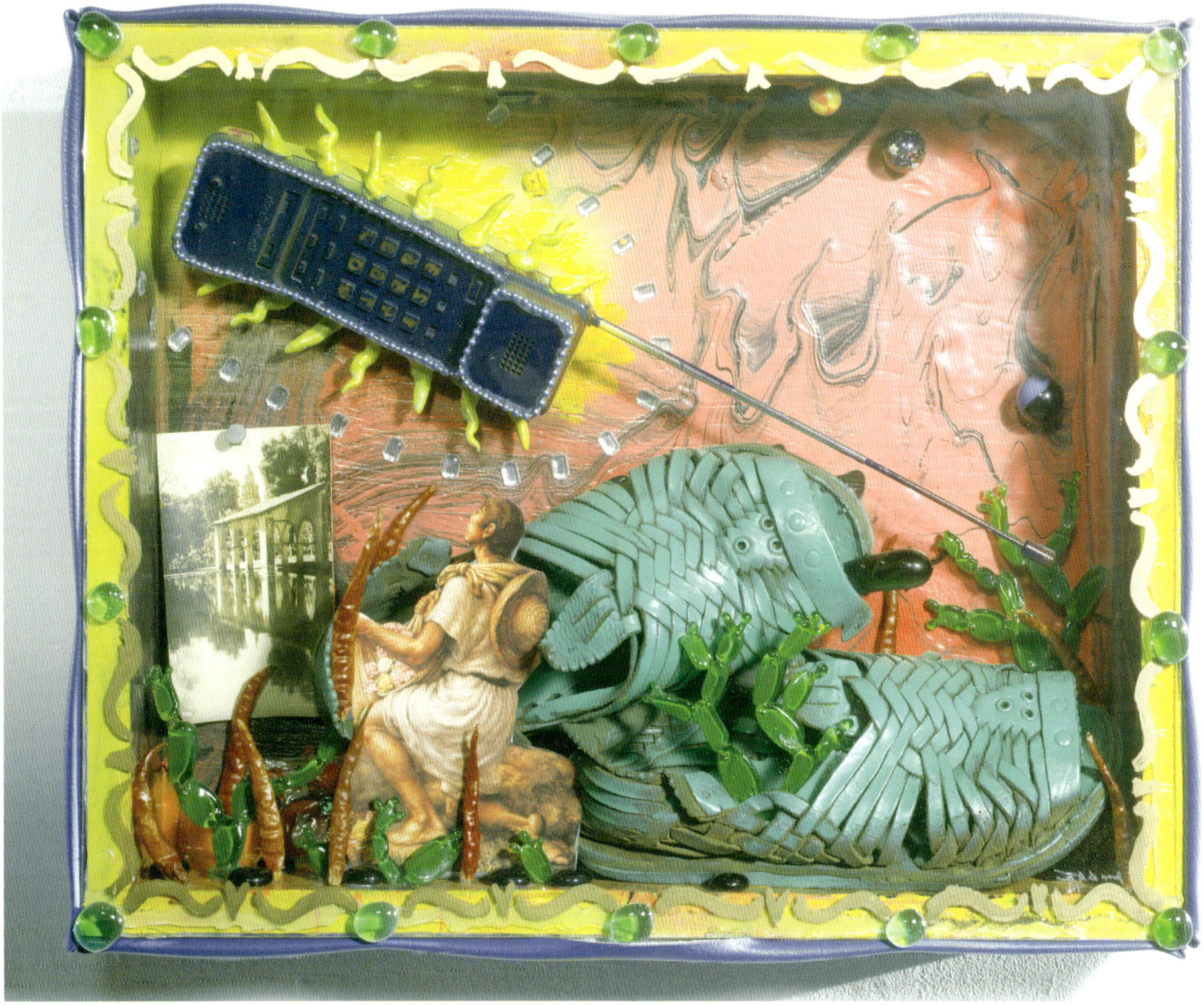

Jamex de la Torre
1-900-VIRGEN, 1996
Mixed media
17 x 21 x 5

The artists would like to thank
John Leighton, Daniel Saxon Gallery, Nora Moore, Mike McGee, Andrea Lee Harris and the Cal State University Art Department.
Glass Students: Jason Chakravarty, Daniel Crawford, Melanie Donegan, Rose Goehner, Wayne Harris, Russ Huff, Robin Provart-Kelly, Manny Krakowski, Sari Ledwith, Carrie McIlwain, Adam Mostow, Gwen Ramstead, Ryan Ross, Mike Tafoya, Hiromi Takizawa, and Greg Vriethoff

Acknowledgments
Dean, College of the Arts, Jerry Samuelson
Chair, Department of Art, Larry Johnson
Director, Main Art Gallery, Mike McGee
Assistant to the Director, Marilyn Moore
Gallery Technician, Martin Lorigan
Exhibition Curator, John Leighton
Installation Assistants: Jason Chakravarty, Dennis Cubbage, Ryan Ross

Exhibition Design Students: April E. Anglin, Janice Christmas, Karen Crews, Dennis Cubbage, Emily Dermenstein, Maria-Lisa Flemington, Sarah Grear, Carlota Haider, Solyi Han, Lori Kameya, Solange K. Ledwith, Milka Marinov, Henry Martinez, Christina Morgan, Michel Oren, Julie Perlin, Cheryl Schriefer, Beth Solomon, Danielle Susalla, Hiromi Takizawa, Ying-su Tang, Diane Winiecki, and Chih-zer Yee.

Exhibition Sponsors:
California State University Fullerton Art Department, College of the Arts; Art Alliance, and the Fund for Instructionally Related Activities

Credits
Photography:
Einar de la Torre: 2,3,4,6,9,10,11,14,18,19,25,28,29,31,34,35,36,38,39,59,62, 68, Marcos Gonzales & Julio Orozco: 24,26,27,30,32,37,42,43,60, Campos Photography: 16,33,41, M.O. Quinn: 5,7,8,12,13,15,17, E.G.Shemp: 44-47,50,67, Jan Wilson: 48,49,58, Dennis Gaxiola: 51, Luis Gutierrez: 52-57, Blue Image Photography: 20,21,22,23,63,64,65,66

Book Design: Andrea Lee Harris
Editors: Sue Henger and Barbara McAlpine
Printed by: Permanent Printing Ltd., Hong Kong
Typeface: LokiCola and Goudy Text

All measurements are listed in inches.
Height and width precedes depth unless otherwise stated.

This book was published by California State University Fullerton Main Art Gallery in collaboration with Grand Central Press for the exhibition, *Fall of Empire*, April 9 – May 14, 2005. Curator John Leighton organized this exhibition with the artists Einar and Jamex de le Torre.

ISBN 0-935314-66-0

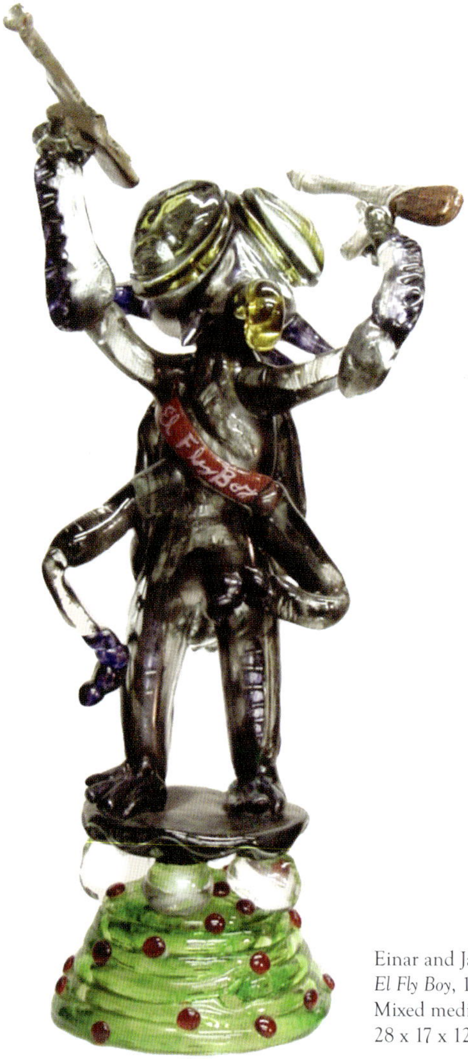

Einar and Jamex collaboration
El Fly Boy, 1999
Mixed media with blown glass
28 x 17 x 12